I Am a Child of God

I AM A CHILD OF GOD
Journal

Faith Favor Future

Faith Favor Future

INNERMISSION PUBLISHING

HAMMOND

FAITH FAVOR FUTURE

The Believer's Proclamation is a statement of who you are and what you can and will do in Christ.

In this companion to **"You are a Child of God-Walking in Faith, Favor, and a Future that is out of the World"** you are given space to write down your thoughts and vision that God gives you as you proclaim who you are in each day.

We should never underestimate the power of "writing down the vision". As you continue to walk as a child of God use this journal as a prayer, vision, or ministry journal to write what God shows you.

This journal has been intentionally formatted in such a way to give you freedom to date, write, and record how best fits your personal style. Make this journal yours and write down your adventure as a **Child of the Most High God!!!**

Dr. J Calaway

Believers Proclamation

Today I am a child of God

I have Faith to Move Mountains

Favor from the King of Kings

And and Future that is out of this World

My Foundation is the Word of God

My Walk is Sure

My Talk is Confident

My Attitude is Like Christ's

Today I will Hear the Word of God

Today I will Do the Will of God

Today I am Convicted, Challenged and Changed

In Jesus Name,

Amen

Start Here

Habakkuk 2:2

Write Down the Vision and Make it Plain

The biggest challenge to living as a child of God is believing you are a child of God. Once you begin to proclaim, "I am a child of God", there is another component to proclamation. Writing your beliefs down. This journal is designed to give you space to write down your beliefs, goals, challenges, and successes.

1. Each section of this journal, the monthly schedule, weekly schedule, and the journal sections are designed to help you succeed at living as a child of God. What you say, where you go, and what you do matters. Your words matter. When you write these things down you are making proclamations of who you are.

2. Preparation is key to living as a *Child of God*. When you prepare your month, weeks, and days ahead of time, you create space for God to guide and direct you.

3. The monthly schedule is designed to provide an overview of your entire month. Take time at the beginning of each month to set goals, establish milestones, and ask God to guide you. Lay your calendar at His feet and ask him to guide you in your schedule. Instead of asking God to bless what you have ordered, ask Him to order your steps and set your schedule according to His guidance.

4. Take time at the beginning of each week (30-60 min) to go over your schedule and goals to evaluate your progress and focus.

5. The weekly schedule is designed to write your daily obligations and appointments.

6. Theme your days. There is an area for you to theme your days. Theming your days gives you a daily focus parameter. This will help you schedule, pray, and focus your energy in specific ways. Set time aside to focus on the specific theme of that day. Daily theme examples:

   1. Family
   2. Finance
   3. Future
   4. Learning/study
   5. Social/Relationship
   6. Career
   7. Self

7. The journal section is designed to guide you through a series of questions to help you write down what you have experienced, accomplished,

envisioned, dreamed, or changed. There are enough sections for you to write one to two days a week or you can write each day. The questions follow the Believers Proclamation so you will be able to see your progress in successfully living as a child of God.

That's it. All you have to do is start. Don't say I'll do it tomorrow, or let me think about it. Just start and watch the motivation catch up to your discipline.

Monthly Calendar

Major Projects/Goals

1. _____
2. _____
3. _____
4. _____
5. _____

Month _____

Sunday	Monday	Tuesday	Wednesday	Thursday	Friday	Saturday

Major Projects/Goals

1. _____
2. _____
3. _____
4. _____
5. _____

Month _____

Sunday	Monday	Tuesday	Wednesday	Thursday	Friday	Saturday

Month _____

Sunday	Monday	Tuesday	Wednesday	Thursday	Friday	Saturday

Major Projects/Goals

1. _____
2. _____
3. _____
4. _____
5. _____

Month _____

Sunday	Monday	Tuesday	Wednesday	Thursday	Friday	Saturday

Major Projects/Goals

1. _____
2. _____
3. _____
4. _____
5. _____

Major Projects/Goals

1. _____
2. _____
3. _____
4. _____
5. _____

Month _____

Sunday	Monday	Tuesday	Wednesday	Thursday	Friday	Saturday

Major Projects/Goals

1. _____
2. _____
3. _____
4. _____
5. _____

Month _____

Sunday	Monday	Tuesday	Wednesday	Thursday	Friday	Saturday

Major Projects/Goals

1. _____
2. _____
3. _____
4. _____
5. _____

Sunday	Monday	Tuesday	Wednesday	Thursday	Friday	Saturday

Month _____

Major Projects/Goals

1. _____
2. _____
3. _____
4. _____
5. _____

Month _____

Sunday	Monday	Tuesday	Wednesday	Thursday	Friday	Saturday

Month _____

Sunday	Monday	Tuesday	Wednesday	Thursday	Friday	Saturday

Major Projects/Goals

1. _____
2. _____
3. _____
4. _____
5. _____

Month _____

Sunday	Monday	Tuesday	Wednesday	Thursday	Friday	Saturday

Major Projects/Goals

1. _____
2. _____
3. _____
4. _____
5. _____

Major Projects/Goals

1. _____

2. _____

3. _____

4. _____

5. _____

Month _____

Sunday	Monday	Tuesday	Wednesday	Thursday	Friday	Saturday

*Month*_____

Sunday	Monday	Tuesday	Wednesday	Thursday	Friday	Saturday

Major Projects/Goals

1. _____
2. _____
3. _____
4. _____
5. _____

Weekly Schedule

Week _____

Date							
Theme							
Time/ Day	Sunday	Monday	Tuesday	Wednesday	Thursday	Friday	Saturday
6am							
7am							
8am							
9am							
10am							
11am							
12pm							
1pm							
2pm							
3pm							
4pm							
5pm							
6pm							
Evening							

Notes/Projects/Goals:

_____

_____

_____

_____

_____

_____

Week _____

Date							
Theme							
Time/Day	Sunday	Monday	Tuesday	Wednesday	Thursday	Friday	Saturday
6am							
7am							
8am							
9am							
10am							
11am							
12pm							
1pm							
2pm							
3pm							
4pm							
5pm							
6pm							
Evening							

Notes/Projects/Goals:

_____
_____
_____
_____
_____
_____

Week _____

Date							
Theme							
Time/Day	Sunday	Monday	Tuesday	Wednesday	Thursday	Friday	Saturday
6am							
7am							
8am							
9am							
10am							
11am							
12pm							
1pm							
2pm							
3pm							
4pm							
5pm							
6pm							
Evening							

Notes/Projects/Goals:

_____
_____
_____
_____
_____
_____

Week _____

Date							
Theme							
Time/Day	Sunday	Monday	Tuesday	Wednesday	Thursday	Friday	Saturday
6am							
7am							
8am							
9am							
10am							
11am							
12pm							
1pm							
2pm							
3pm							
4pm							
5pm							
6pm							
Evening							

Notes/Projects/Goals:

_____
_____
_____
_____
_____
_____

Week _____

Date							
Theme							
Time/ Day	Sunday	Monday	Tuesday	Wednesday	Thursday	Friday	Saturday
6am							
7am							
8am							
9am							
10am							
11am							
12pm							
1pm							
2pm							
3pm							
4pm							
5pm							
6pm							
Evening							

Notes/Projects/Goals:

_____

_____

_____

_____

_____

_____

Week _____

Date							
Theme							
Time/Day	Sunday	Monday	Tuesday	Wednesday	Thursday	Friday	Saturday
6am							
7am							
8am							
9am							
10am							
11am							
12pm							
1pm							
2pm							
3pm							
4pm							
5pm							
6pm							
Evening							

Notes/Projects/Goals:

_____
_____
_____
_____
_____
_____

Week _____

Date							
Theme							
Time/Day	Sunday	Monday	Tuesday	Wednesday	Thursday	Friday	Saturday
6am							
7am							
8am							
9am							
10am							
11am							
12pm							
1pm							
2pm							
3pm							
4pm							
5pm							
6pm							
Evening							

Notes/Projects/Goals:

_____
_____
_____
_____
_____
_____

Week _____

Date							
Theme							
Time/ Day	Sunday	Monday	Tuesday	Wednesday	Thursday	Friday	Saturday
6am							
7am							
8am							
9am							
10am							
11am							
12pm							
1pm							
2pm							
3pm							
4pm							
5pm							
6pm							
Evening							

Notes/Projects/Goals:

_____
_____
_____
_____
_____
_____

Week _____

Date							
Theme							
Time/ Day	Sunday	Monday	Tuesday	Wednesday	Thursday	Friday	Saturday
6am							
7am							
8am							
9am							
10am							
11am							
12pm							
1pm							
2pm							
3pm							
4pm							
5pm							
6pm							
Evening							

Notes/Projects/Goals:

_____
_____
_____
_____
_____
_____

Week _____

Date							
Theme							
Time/Day	Sunday	Monday	Tuesday	Wednesday	Thursday	Friday	Saturday
6am							
7am							
8am							
9am							
10am							
11am							
12m							
1pm							
2pm							
3pm							
4pm							
5pm							
6pm							
Evening							

Notes/Projects/Goals:

_____
_____
_____
_____
_____
_____

Week _____

Date							
Theme							
Time/ Day	Sunday	Monday	Tuesday	Wednesday	Thursday	Friday	Saturday
6am							
7am							
8am							
9am							
10am							
11am							
12pm							
1pm							
2pm							
3pm							
4pm							
5pm							
6pm							
Evening							

Notes/Projects/Goals:

_____

_____

_____

_____

_____

_____

Week _____

Date							
Theme							
Time/Day	Sunday	Monday	Tuesday	Wednesday	Thursday	Friday	Saturday
6am							
7am							
8am							
9am							
10am							
11am							
12pm							
1pm							
2pm							
3pm							
4pm							
5pm							
6pm							
Evening							

Notes/Projects/Goals:

_____
_____
_____
_____
_____
_____

Week _____

Date							
Theme							
Time/Day	Sunday	Monday	Tuesday	Wednesday	Thursday	Friday	Saturday
6am							
7am							
8am							
9am							
10am							
11am							
12pm							
1pm							
2pm							
3pm							
4pm							
5pm							
6pm							
Evening							

Notes/Projects/Goals:

_____
_____
_____
_____
_____
_____

Week _____

Date							
Theme							
Time/ Day	Sunday	Monday	Tuesday	Wednesday	Thursday	Friday	Saturday
6am							
7am							
8am							
9am							
10am							
11am							
12am							
1pm							
2pm							
3pm							
4pm							
5pm							
6pm							
Evening							

Notes/Projects/Goals:

_____
_____
_____
_____
_____
_____

Week _____

Date							
Theme							
Time/Day	Sunday	Monday	Tuesday	Wednesday	Thursday	Friday	Saturday
6am							
7am							
8am							
9am							
10am							
11am							
12pm							
1pm							
2pm							
3pm							
4pm							
5pm							
6pm							
Evening							

Notes/Projects/Goals:

_____

_____

_____

_____

_____

_____

Week _____

Date							
Theme							
Time/Day	Sunday	Monday	Tuesday	Wednesday	Thursday	Friday	Saturday
6am							
7am							
8am							
9am							
10am							
11am							
12pm							
1pm							
2pm							
3pm							
4pm							
5pm							
6pm							
Evening							

Notes/Projects/Goals:

_____
_____
_____
_____
_____
_____

Week _____

Date							
Theme							
Time/Day	Sunday	Monday	Tuesday	Wednesday	Thursday	Friday	Saturday
6am							
7am							
8am							
9am							
10am							
11am							
12pm							
1pm							
2pm							
3pm							
4pm							
5pm							
6pm							
Evening							

Notes/Projects/Goals:

_____

_____

_____

_____

_____

_____

Week _____

Date							
Theme							
Time/ Day	Sunday	Monday	Tuesday	Wednesday	Thursday	Friday	Saturday
6am							
7am							
8am							
9am							
10am							
11am							
12pm							
1pm							
2pm							
3pm							
4pm							
5pm							
6pm							
Evening							

Notes/Projects/Goals:

_____

_____

_____

_____

_____

_____

Week _____

Date							
Theme							
Time/Day	Sunday	Monday	Tuesday	Wednesday	Thursday	Friday	Saturday
6am							
7am							
8am							
9am							
10am							
11am							
12pm							
1pm							
2pm							
3pm							
4pm							
5pm							
6pm							
Evening							

Notes/Projects/Goals:

_____

_____

_____

_____

_____

_____

Week _____

Date							
Theme							
Time/Day	Sunday	Monday	Tuesday	Wednesday	Thursday	Friday	Saturday
6am							
7am							
8am							
9am							
10am							
11am							
12pm							
1pm							
2pm							
3pm							
4pm							
5pm							
6pm							
Evening							

Notes/Projects/Goals:

_____
_____
_____
_____
_____
_____

Week _____

Time/Day	Sunday	Monday	Tuesday	Wednesday	Thursday	Friday	Saturday
Date							
Theme							
6am							
7am							
8am							
9am							
10am							
11am							
12pm							
1pm							
2pm							
3pm							
4pm							
5pm							
6pm							
Evening							

Notes/Projects/Goals:

_____

_____

_____

_____

_____

_____

Week _____

Date							
Theme							
Time/Day	Sunday	Monday	Tuesday	Wednesday	Thursday	Friday	Saturday
6am							
7am							
8am							
9am							
10am							
11am							
12pm							
1pm							
2pm							
3pm							
4pm							
5pm							
6pm							
Evening							

Notes/Projects/Goals:

_____
_____
_____
_____
_____
_____

Week _____

Date							
Theme							
Time/Day	Sunday	Monday	Tuesday	Wednesday	Thursday	Friday	Saturday
6am							
7am							
8am							
9am							
10am							
11am							
12pm							
1pm							
2pm							
3pm							
4pm							
5pm							
6pm							
Evening							

Notes/Projects/Goals:

_____

_____

_____

_____

_____

_____

Week _____

Date							
Theme							
Time/Day	Sunday	Monday	Tuesday	Wednesday	Thursday	Friday	Saturday
6am							
7am							
a8am							
9am							
10am							
11am							
12pm							
1pm							
2pm							
3pm							
4pm							
5pm							
6pm							
Evening							

Notes/Projects/Goals:

_____
_____
_____
_____
_____
_____

Week _____

Date							
Theme							
Time/Day	Sunday	Monday	Tuesday	Wednesday	Thursday	Friday	Saturday
6am							
7am							
8am							
9am							
10am							
11am							
12pm							
1pm							
2pm							
3pm							
4pm							
5pm							
6pm							
Evening							

Notes/Projects/Goals:

_____
_____
_____
_____
_____
_____

Week _____

Date							
Theme							
Time/ Day	Sunday	Monday	Tuesday	Wednesday	Thursday	Friday	Saturday
6am							
7am							
8am							
9am							
10am							
11am							
12pm							
1pm							
2pm							
3pm							
4pm							
5pm							
6pm							
Evening							

Notes/Projects/Goals:

_____
_____
_____
_____
_____
_____

Week _____

Date							
Theme							
Time/Day	Sunday	Monday	Tuesday	Wednesday	Thursday	Friday	Saturday
6am							
7am							
8am							
9am							
10am							
11am							
12pm							
1pm							
2pm							
3pm							
4pm							
5pm							
6pm							
Evening							

Notes/Projects/Goals:

_____
_____
_____
_____
_____
_____

Week _____

Date							
Theme							
Time/Day	Sunday	Monday	Tuesday	Wednesday	Thursday	Friday	Saturday
6am							
7am							
8am							
9am							
10am							
11am							
12pm							
1pm							
2pm							
3pm							
4pm							
5pm							
6pm							
Evening							

Notes/Projects/Goals:

_____
_____
_____
_____
_____
_____

Week _____

Date							
Theme							
Time/Day	Sunday	Monday	Tuesday	Wednesday	Thursday	Friday	Saturday
6am							
7am							
8am							
9am							
10am							
11am							
12pm							
1pm							
2pm							
3pm							
4pm							
5pm							
6pm							
Evening							

Notes/Projects/Goals:

_____
_____
_____
_____
_____
_____

Week _____

Date							
Theme							
Time/ Date	Sunday	Monday	Tuesday	Wednesday	Thursday	Friday	Saturday
6am							
7am							
8am							
9am							
10am							
11am							
12pm							
1pm							
2pm							
3pm							
4pm							
5pm							
6pm							
Evening							

Notes/Projects/Goals:

_____

_____

_____

_____

_____

_____

Week _____

Date							
Theme							
Time/ Date	Sunday	Monday	Tuesday	Wednesday	Thursday	Friday	Saturday
6am							
7am							
8am							
9am							
10am							
11am							
12pm							
1pm							
2pm							
3pm							
4pm							
5pm							
6pm							
Evening							

Notes/Projects/Goals:

_____

_____

_____

_____

_____

_____

Week _____

Date							
Theme							
Time/Day	Sunday	Monday	Tuesday	Wednesday	Thursday	Friday	Saturday
6am							
7am							
8am							
9am							
10am							
11am							
12pm							
1pm							
2pm							
3pm							
4pm							
5pm							
6pm							
Evening							

Notes/Projects/Goals:

_____
_____
_____
_____
_____
_____

Week _____

Date							
Theme							
Time/ Day	Sunday	Monday	Tuesday	Wednesday	Thursday	Friday	Saturday
6am							
7am							
8am							
9am							
10am							
11am							
12pm							
1pm							
2pm							
3pm							
4pm							
5pm							
6pm							
Evening							

Notes/Projects/Goals:

_____
_____
_____
_____
_____
_____

Week _____

Date							
Theme							
Time/Day	Sunday	Monday	Tuesday	Wednesday	Thursday	Friday	Saturday
6am							
7am							
8am							
9am							
10am							
11am							
12pm							
1pm							
2pm							
3pm							
4pm							
5pm							
6pm							
Evening							

Notes/Projects/Goals:

_____
_____
_____
_____
_____
_____

Week _____

Time/Day	Sunday	Monday	Tuesday	Wednesday	Thursday	Friday	Saturday
Date							
Theme							
6am							
7am							
8am							
9am							
10am							
11am							
12pm							
1pm							
2pm							
3pm							
4pm							
5pm							
6pm							
Evening							

Notes/Projects/Goals:

_____

_____

_____

_____

_____

_____

Week _____

Date							
Theme							
Time/ Day	Sunday	Monday	Tuesday	Wednesday	Thursday	Friday	Saturday
6am							
7am							
8am							
9am							
10am							
11am							
12pm							
1pm							
2pm							
3pm							
4pm							
5pm							
6pm							
Evening							

Notes/Projects/Goals:

_____

_____

_____

_____

_____

_____

Week _____

Date							
Theme							
Time/Day	Sunday	Monday	Tuesday	Wednesday	Thursday	Friday	Saturday
6am							
7am							
8am							
9am							
10am							
11am							
12pm							
1pm							
2pm							
3pm							
4pm							
5pm							
6pm							
Evening							

Notes/Projects/Goals:

_____
_____
_____
_____
_____
_____

Week _____

Date							
Theme							
Time/Day	Sunday	Monday	Tuesday	Wednesday	Thursday	Friday	Saturday
6am							
7am							
8am							
9am							
10am							
11am							
12pm							
1pm							
2pm							
3pm							
4pm							
5pm							
6pm							
Evening							

Notes/Projects/Goals:

_____

_____

_____

_____

_____

_____

Week _____

Date							
Theme							
Time/ Day	Sunday	Monday	Tuesday	Wednesday	Thursday	Friday	Saturday
6am							
7am							
8am							
9am							
10am							
11am							
12pm							
1pm							
2pm							
3pm							
4pm							
5pm							
6pm							
Evening							

Notes/Projects/Goals:

_____
_____
_____
_____
_____
_____

Week _____

Date							
Theme							
Time/Day	Sunday	Monday	Tuesday	Wednesday	Thursday	Friday	Saturday
6am							
7am							
8am							
9am							
10am							
11am							
12pm							
1pm							
2pm							
3pm							
4pm							
5pm							
6pm							
Evening							

Notes/Projects/Goals:

_____
_____
_____
_____
_____
_____

Week _____

Date							
Theme							
Time/ Day	Sunday	Monday	Tuesday	Wednesday	Thursday	Friday	Saturday
6am							
7am							
9am							
9am							
10am							
11am							
12pm							
1pm							
2pm							
3pm							
4pm							
5pm							
6pm							
Evening							

Notes/Projects/Goals:

_____

_____

_____

_____

_____

_____

Week _____

Date							
Theme							
Time/ Day	Sunday	Monday	Tuesday	Wednesday	Thursday	Friday	Saturday
6am							
7am							
8am							
9am							
10am							
11am							
12pm							
1pm							
2pm							
3pm							
4pm							
5pm							
6pm							
Evening							

Notes/Projects/Goals:

_____
_____
_____
_____
_____
_____

Week _____

Date							
Theme							
Time/Day	Sunday	Monday	Tuesday	Wednesday	Thursday	Friday	Saturday
6am							
7am							
8am							
9am							
10am							
11am							
12pm							
1pm							
2pm							
3pm							
4pm							
5pm							
6pm							
Evening							

Notes/Projects/Goals:

_____

_____

_____

_____

_____

_____

Week _____

Time/Day	Sunday	Monday	Tuesday	Wednesday	Thursday	Friday	Saturday
Date							
Theme							
6am							
7am							
8am							
9am							
10am							
11am							
12pm							
1pm							
2pm							
3pm							
4pm							
5pm							
6pm							
Evening							

Notes/Projects/Goals:

_____
_____
_____
_____
_____
_____

Week _____

Date							
Theme							
Time/Date	Sunday	Monday	Tuesday	Wednesday	Thursday	Friday	Saturday
6am							
7am							
8am							
9am							
10am							
11am							
12pm							
1pm							
2pm							
3pm							
4pm							
5pm							
6pm							
Evening							

Notes/Projects/Goals:

_____
_____
_____
_____
_____
_____

Week _____

Time/Day	Sunday	Monday	Tuesday	Wednesday	Thursday	Friday	Saturday
Date							
Theme							
6am							
7am							
8am							
9am							
10am							
11am							
12pm							
1pm							
2pm							
3pm							
4pm							
5pm							
6pm							
Evening							

Notes/Projects/Goals:

_____
_____
_____
_____
_____
_____

Week _____

Date							
Theme							
Time/ Day	Sunday	Monday	Tuesday	Wednesday	Thursday	Friday	Saturday
6am							
7am							
8am							
9am							
10am							
11am							
12pm							
1pm							
2pm							
3pm							
4pm							
5pm							
6pm							
Evening							

Notes/Projects/Goals:

_____

_____

_____

_____

_____

_____

Week _____

Time/Day	Sunday	Monday	Tuesday	Wednesday	Thursday	Friday	Saturday
Date							
Theme							
6am							
7am							
8am							
9am							
10am							
11am							
12pm							
1pm							
2pm							
3pm							
4pm							
5pm							
6pm							
Evening							

Notes/Projects/Goals:

_____
_____
_____
_____
_____
_____

Week _____

Date							
Theme							
Time/Day	Sunday	Monday	Tuesday	Wednesday	Thursday	Friday	Saturday
6am							
7am							
8am							
9am							
10am							
11am							
12am							
1pm							
2pm							
3pm							
4pm							
5pm							
6pm							
Evening							

Notes/Projects/Goals:

_____

_____

_____

_____

_____

_____

Week _____

Date							
Theme							
Time/ Date	Sunday	Monday	Tuesday	Wednesday	Thursday	Friday	Saturday
6am							
7am							
8am							
9am							
10am							
11am							
12pm							
1pm							
2pm							
3pm							
4pm							
5pm							
6pm							
Evening							

Notes/Projects/Goals:

_____
_____
_____
_____
_____
_____

Week _____

Date							
Theme							
Time/Date	Sunday	Monday	Tuesday	Wednesday	Thursday	Friday	Saturday
6am							
7am							
8am							
9am							
10am							
11am							
12pm							
1pm							
2pm							
3pm							
4pm							
5pm							
6pm							
Evening							

Notes/Projects/Goals:

_____
_____
_____
_____
_____
_____

Week _____

Date							
Theme							
Time/ Day	Sunday	Monday	Tuesday	Wednesday	Thursday	Friday	Saturday
6am							
7am							
8am							
9am							
10am							
11am							
12pm							
1pm							
2pm							
3pm							
4pm							
5pm							
6pm							
Evening							

Notes/Projects/Goals:

_____
_____
_____
_____
_____
_____

I am a Child of God

Journal

Date ___/___/___

Today I am a Child of God

Write a proclamation of belief. Each time you write, you are ensuring your vision and beliefs will carry on to the next generation.

_____

_____

_____

_____

_____

_____

_____

_____

_____

_____

How has my belief dictated my behavior today? (Faith)

_____

_____

_____

_____

_____

_____

_____

How was I favored/How did I show favor? (Favor)

_____

_____

_____

_____

_____

_____

_____

What have I done to secure my future/What are My goals? (Future)

_____

_____

_____

_____

_____

_____

How have I stood firm in my walk and words? (Foundation/Walk/ Talk)

_____

_____

_____

_____

_____

_____

How have I displayed Christ's attitude/Where can I improve? (Attitude)

_____

_____

_____

_____

_____
_____

What Have I listened to that has stood out? (Hear)

_____
_____
_____
_____
_____
_____
_____

What have I accomplished? (Do)

_____
_____
_____
_____
_____
_____
_____

How have I changed/am changing? (Convicted/Challenged/Changed)

_____
_____
_____
_____
_____
_____
_____

Date ___/___/___

Today I am a Child of God

Write a proclamation of belief. Each time you write, you are ensuring your vision and beliefs will carry on to the next generation.

_____
_____
_____
_____
_____
_____
_____
_____
_____
_____

How has my belief dictated my behavior today? (Faith)

_____
_____
_____
_____
_____
_____

How was I favored/How did I show favor? (Favor)

_____
_____
_____
_____

_____

_____

_____

*What have I done to secure my future/What are My goals?
(Future)*

_____

_____

_____

_____

_____

_____

_____

*How have I stood firm in my walk and words? (Foundation/Walk/
Talk)*

_____

_____

_____

_____

_____

_____

_____

*How have I displayed Christ's attitude/Where can I improve?
(Attitude)*

_____

_____

_____

_____

_____

_____
_____

What Have I listened to that has stood out? (Hear)

_____
_____
_____
_____
_____
_____

What have I accomplished? (Do)

_____
_____
_____
_____
_____
_____

How have I changed/am changing? (Convicted/Challenged/ Changed)

_____
_____
_____
_____
_____
_____

Date ___/___/___

Today I am a Child of God

Write a proclamation of belief. Each time you write, you are ensuring your vision and beliefs will carry on to the next generation.

_____
_____
_____
_____
_____
_____
_____
_____
_____
_____

How has my belief dictated my behavior today? (Faith)

_____
_____
_____
_____
_____
_____
_____

How was I favored/How did I show favor? (Favor)

_____
_____
_____
_____

_____

_____

_____

What have I done to secure my future/What are My goals? (Future)

_____

_____

_____

_____

_____

_____

_____

How have I stood firm in my walk and words? (Foundation/Walk/ Talk)

_____

_____

_____

_____

_____

_____

How have I displayed Christ's attitude/Where can I improve? (Attitude)

_____

_____

_____

_____

_____

_____

What Have I listened to that has stood out? (Hear)

_____

_____

_____

_____

_____

_____

What have I accomplished? (Do)

_____

_____

_____

_____

_____

_____

How have I changed/am changing? (Convicted/Challenged/ Changed)

_____

_____

_____

_____

_____

_____

Date ___/___/___

Today I am a Child of God

Write a proclamation of belief. Each time you write, you are ensuring your vision and beliefs will carry on to the next generation.

_____
_____
_____
_____
_____
_____
_____
_____
_____
_____

How has my belief dictated my behavior today? (Faith)

_____
_____
_____
_____
_____
_____
_____

How was I favored/How did I show favor? (Favor)

_____
_____
_____
_____

_____

_____

_____

What have I done to secure my future/What are My goals? (Future)

_____

_____

_____

_____

_____

_____

_____

How have I stood firm in my walk and words? (Foundation/Walk/ Talk)

_____

_____

_____

_____

_____

_____

How have I displayed Christ's attitude/Where can I improve? (Attitude)

_____

_____

_____

_____

_____

_____
_____

What Have I listened to that has stood out? (Hear)

_____
_____
_____
_____
_____
_____

What have I accomplished? (Do)

_____
_____
_____
_____
_____
_____

How have I changed/am changing? (Convicted/Challenged/ Changed)

_____
_____
_____
_____
_____
_____

Date ___/___/___

Today I am a Child of God

Write a proclamation of belief. Each time you write, you are ensuring your vision and beliefs will carry on to the next generation.

_____

_____

_____

_____

_____

_____

_____

_____

_____

_____

How has my belief dictated my behavior today? (Faith)

_____

_____

_____

_____

_____

_____

How was I favored/How did I show favor? (Favor)

_____

_____

_____

_____

_____

_____

_____

What have I done to secure my future/What are My goals? (Future)

_____

_____

_____

_____

_____

_____

_____

How have I stood firm in my walk and words? (Foundation/Walk/ Talk)

_____

_____

_____

_____

_____

_____

_____

How have I displayed Christ's attitude/Where can I improve? (Attitude)

_____

_____

_____

_____

_____

_____

_____

What Have I listened to that has stood out? (Hear)

_____

_____

_____

_____

_____

_____

What have I accomplished? (Do)

_____

_____

_____

_____

_____

_____

How have I changed/am changing? (Convicted/Challenged/ Changed)

_____

_____

_____

_____

_____

_____

Date ___/___/___

Today I am a Child of God

Write a proclamation of belief. Each time you write, you are ensuring your vision and beliefs will carry on to the next generation.

_____
_____
_____
_____
_____
_____
_____
_____
_____
_____

How has my belief dictated my behavior today? (Faith)

_____
_____
_____
_____
_____
_____

How was I favored/How did I show favor? (Favor)

_____
_____
_____
_____

_____
_____
_____

What have I done to secure my future/What are My goals?
(Future)

_____
_____
_____
_____
_____
_____
_____

How have I stood firm in my walk and words? (Foundation/Walk/
Talk)

_____
_____
_____
_____
_____
_____
_____

How have I displayed Christ's attitude/Where can I improve?
(Attitude)

_____
_____
_____
_____
_____

_____

_____

What Have I listened to that has stood out? (Hear)

_____

_____

_____

_____

_____

_____

What have I accomplished? (Do)

_____

_____

_____

_____

_____

_____

How have I changed/am changing? (Convicted/Challenged/ Changed)

_____

_____

_____

_____

_____

_____

Date ___/___/___

Today I am a Child of God

Write a proclamation of belief. Each time you write, you are ensuring your vision and beliefs will carry on to the next generation.

_____

_____

_____

_____

_____

_____

_____

_____

_____

_____

How has my belief dictated my behavior today? (Faith)

_____

_____

_____

_____

_____

_____

How was I favored/How did I show favor? (Favor)

_____

_____

_____

_____

_____

_____

What have I done to secure my future/What are My goals? (Future)

_____

_____

_____

_____

_____

_____

How have I stood firm in my walk and words? (Foundation/Walk/ Talk)

_____

_____

_____

_____

_____

_____

How have I displayed Christ's attitude/Where can I improve? (Attitude)

_____

_____

_____

_____

_____

_____
_____

What Have I listened to that has stood out? (Hear)

_____
_____
_____
_____
_____
_____
_____

What have I accomplished? (Do)

_____
_____
_____
_____
_____
_____
_____

How have I changed/am changing? (Convicted/Challenged/ Changed)

_____
_____
_____
_____
_____
_____
_____

Date ___/___/___

Today I am a Child of God

Write a proclamation of belief. Each time you write, you are ensuring your vision and beliefs will carry on to the next generation.

_____
_____
_____
_____
_____
_____
_____
_____
_____
_____

How has my belief dictated my behavior today? (Faith)

_____
_____
_____
_____
_____
_____

How was I favored/How did I show favor? (Favor)

_____
_____
_____
_____

_____

_____

_____

What have I done to secure my future/What are My goals? (Future)

_____

_____

_____

_____

_____

_____

_____

How have I stood firm in my walk and words? (Foundation/Walk/ Talk)

_____

_____

_____

_____

_____

_____

How have I displayed Christ's attitude/Where can I improve? (Attitude)

_____

_____

_____

_____

What Have I listened to that has stood out? (Hear)

_____
_____
_____
_____
_____
_____

What have I accomplished? (Do)

_____
_____
_____
_____
_____
_____

How have I changed/am changing? (Convicted/Challenged/ Changed)

_____
_____
_____
_____
_____
_____

Date ___/___/___

Today I am a Child of God

Write a proclamation of belief. Each time you write, you are ensuring your vision and beliefs will carry on to the next generation.

_____

_____

_____

_____

_____

_____

_____

_____

_____

_____

How has my belief dictated my behavior today? (Faith)

_____

_____

_____

_____

_____

_____

How was I favored/How did I show favor? (Favor)

_____

_____

_____

_____

_____

_____

What have I done to secure my future/What are My goals? (Future)

_____

_____

_____

_____

_____

_____

How have I stood firm in my walk and words? (Foundation/Walk/ Talk)

_____

_____

_____

_____

_____

_____

How have I displayed Christ's attitude/Where can I improve? (Attitude)

_____

_____

_____

_____

_____

_____

_____

What Have I listened to that has stood out? (Hear)

_____

_____

_____

_____

_____

_____

What have I accomplished? (Do)

_____

_____

_____

_____

_____

_____

How have I changed/am changing? (Convicted/Challenged/Changed)

_____

_____

_____

_____

_____

_____

Date ___/___/___

Today I am a Child of God

Write a proclamation of belief. Each time you write, you are ensuring your vision and beliefs will carry on to the next generation.

_____
_____
_____
_____
_____
_____
_____
_____
_____
_____

How has my belief dictated my behavior today? (Faith)

_____
_____
_____
_____
_____
_____
_____

How was I favored/How did I show favor? (Favor)

_____
_____
_____
_____

_____

_____

_____

What have I done to secure my future/What are My goals? (Future)

_____

_____

_____

_____

_____

_____

_____

How have I stood firm in my walk and words? (Foundation/Walk/ Talk)

_____

_____

_____

_____

_____

_____

_____

How have I displayed Christ's attitude/Where can I improve? (Attitude)

_____

_____

_____

_____

_____

_____

_____

What Have I listened to that has stood out? (Hear)

_____

_____

_____

_____

_____

_____

What have I accomplished? (Do)

_____

_____

_____

_____

_____

_____

How have I changed/am changing? (Convicted/Challenged/ Changed)

_____

_____

_____

_____

_____

_____

Date ___/___/___

Today I am a Child of God

Write a proclamation of belief. Each time you write, you are ensuring your vision and beliefs will carry on to the next generation.

_____

_____

_____

_____

_____

_____

_____

_____

_____

How has my belief dictated my behavior today? (Faith)

_____

_____

_____

_____

_____

_____

How was I favored/How did I show favor? (Favor)

_____

_____

_____

_____

_____

_____

What have I done to secure my future/What are My goals? (Future)

_____

_____

_____

_____

_____

_____

_____

How have I stood firm in my walk and words? (Foundation/Walk/ Talk)

_____

_____

_____

_____

_____

_____

_____

How have I displayed Christ's attitude/Where can I improve? (Attitude)

_____

_____

_____

_____

_____

_____

_____

What Have I listened to that has stood out? (Hear)

_____

_____

_____

_____

_____

_____

_____

What have I accomplished? (Do)

_____

_____

_____

_____

_____

_____

How have I changed/am changing? (Convicted/Challenged/Changed)

_____

_____

_____

_____

_____

_____

Date ___/___/___

Today I am a Child of God

Write a proclamation of belief. Each time you write, you are ensuring your vision and beliefs will carry on to the next generation.

_____
_____
_____
_____
_____
_____
_____
_____
_____
_____

How has my belief dictated my behavior today? (Faith)

_____
_____
_____
_____
_____
_____
_____

How was I favored/How did I show favor? (Favor)

_____
_____
_____
_____

_____

_____

_____

What have I done to secure my future/What are My goals? (Future)

_____

_____

_____

_____

_____

_____

_____

How have I stood firm in my walk and words? (Foundation/Walk/ Talk)

_____

_____

_____

_____

_____

_____

_____

How have I displayed Christ's attitude/Where can I improve? (Attitude)

_____

_____

_____

_____

_____

_____

_____

What Have I listened to that has stood out? (Hear)

_____

_____

_____

_____

_____

_____

_____

What have I accomplished? (Do)

_____

_____

_____

_____

_____

_____

_____

How have I changed/am changing? (Convicted/Challenged/ Changed)

_____

_____

_____

_____

_____

_____

_____

Date ___/___/___

Today I am a Child of God

Write a proclamation of belief. Each time you write, you are ensuring your vision and beliefs will carry on to the next generation.

_____

_____

_____

_____

_____

_____

_____

_____

_____

_____

How has my belief dictated my behavior today? (Faith)

_____

_____

_____

_____

_____

_____

_____

How was I favored/How did I show favor? (Favor)

_____

_____

_____

_____

_____

_____

_____

What have I done to secure my future/What are My goals? (Future)

_____

_____

_____

_____

_____

_____

How have I stood firm in my walk and words? (Foundation/Walk/ Talk)

_____

_____

_____

_____

_____

_____

How have I displayed Christ's attitude/Where can I improve? (Attitude)

_____

_____

_____

_____

_____

_____

_____

What Have I listened to that has stood out? (Hear)

_____

_____

_____

_____

_____

_____

_____

What have I accomplished? (Do)

_____

_____

_____

_____

_____

_____

_____

*How have I changed/am changing? (Convicted/Challenged/
Changed)*

_____

_____

_____

_____

_____

_____

_____

Date ___/___/___

Today I am a Child of God

Write a proclamation of belief. Each time you write, you are ensuring your vision and beliefs will carry on to the next generation.

_____
_____
_____
_____
_____
_____
_____
_____
_____

How has my belief dictated my behavior today? (Faith)

_____
_____
_____
_____
_____
_____

How was I favored/How did I show favor? (Favor)

_____
_____
_____
_____

_____

_____

_____

What have I done to secure my future/What are My goals? (Future)

_____

_____

_____

_____

_____

_____

_____

How have I stood firm in my walk and words? (Foundation/Walk/ Talk)

_____

_____

_____

_____

_____

_____

How have I displayed Christ's attitude/Where can I improve? (Attitude)

_____

_____

_____

_____

_____

_____
_____

What Have I listened to that has stood out? (Hear)

_____
_____
_____
_____
_____
_____

What have I accomplished? (Do)

_____
_____
_____
_____
_____
_____

How have I changed/am changing? (Convicted/Challenged/ Changed)

_____
_____
_____
_____
_____
_____

Date ___/___/___

Today I am a Child of God

Write a proclamation of belief. Each time you write, you are ensuring your vision and beliefs will carry on to the next generation.

_____

_____

_____

_____

_____

_____

_____

_____

_____

_____

How has my belief dictated my behavior today? (Faith)

_____

_____

_____

_____

_____

_____

_____

How was I favored/How did I show favor? (Favor)

_____

_____

_____

_____

_____

_____

_____

What have I done to secure my future/What are My goals? (Future)

_____

_____

_____

_____

_____

_____

_____

How have I stood firm in my walk and words? (Foundation/Walk/ Talk)

_____

_____

_____

_____

_____

_____

_____

How have I displayed Christ's attitude/Where can I improve? (Attitude)

_____

_____

_____

_____

_____

_____

_____

What Have I listened to that has stood out? (Hear)

_____

_____

_____

_____

_____

_____

_____

What have I accomplished? (Do)

_____

_____

_____

_____

_____

_____

_____

How have I changed/am changing? (Convicted/Challenged/ Changed)

_____

_____

_____

_____

_____

_____

_____

Date ___/___/___

Today I am a Child of God

Write a proclamation of belief. Each time you write, you are ensuring your vision and beliefs will carry on to the next generation.

_____
_____
_____
_____
_____
_____
_____
_____
_____

How has my belief dictated my behavior today? (Faith)

_____
_____
_____
_____
_____
_____

How was I favored/How did I show favor? (Favor)

_____
_____
_____
_____

_____
_____
_____

What have I done to secure my future/What are My goals? (Future)

_____
_____
_____
_____
_____
_____
_____

How have I stood firm in my walk and words? (Foundation/Walk/ Talk)

_____
_____
_____
_____
_____
_____
_____

How have I displayed Christ's attitude/Where can I improve? (Attitude)

_____
_____
_____
_____
_____

_____

_____

What Have I listened to that has stood out? (Hear)

_____

_____

_____

_____

_____

_____

_____

What have I accomplished? (Do)

_____

_____

_____

_____

_____

_____

How have I changed/am changing? (Convicted/Challenged/ Changed)

_____

_____

_____

_____

_____

_____

_____

Date ___/___/___

Today I am a Child of God

Write a proclamation of belief. Each time you write, you are ensuring your vision and beliefs will carry on to the next generation.

_____
_____
_____
_____
_____
_____
_____
_____
_____
_____

How has my belief dictated my behavior today? (Faith)

_____
_____
_____
_____
_____
_____
_____

How was I favored/How did I show favor? (Favor)

_____
_____
_____
_____

_____
_____
_____

What have I done to secure my future/What are My goals? (Future)

_____
_____
_____
_____
_____
_____

How have I stood firm in my walk and words? (Foundation/Walk/ Talk)

_____
_____
_____
_____
_____
_____

How have I displayed Christ's attitude/Where can I improve? (Attitude)

_____
_____
_____
_____

What Have I listened to that has stood out? (Hear)

_____

_____

_____

_____

_____

_____

What have I accomplished? (Do)

_____

_____

_____

_____

_____

_____

How have I changed/am changing? (Convicted/Challenged/Changed)

_____

_____

_____

_____

_____

_____

Date ___/___/___

Today I am a Child of God

Write a proclamation of belief. Each time you write, you are ensuring your vision and beliefs will carry on to the next generation.

_____
_____
_____
_____
_____
_____
_____
_____
_____
_____

How has my belief dictated my behavior today? (Faith)

_____
_____
_____
_____
_____
_____

How was I favored/How did I show favor? (Favor)

_____
_____
_____
_____

_____

_____

_____

What have I done to secure my future/What are My goals? (Future)

_____

_____

_____

_____

_____

_____

_____

How have I stood firm in my walk and words? (Foundation/Walk/ Talk)

_____

_____

_____

_____

_____

_____

How have I displayed Christ's attitude/Where can I improve? (Attitude)

_____

_____

_____

_____

_____

_____

_____

What Have I listened to that has stood out? (Hear)

_____

_____

_____

_____

_____

_____

_____

What have I accomplished? (Do)

_____

_____

_____

_____

_____

_____

_____

How have I changed/am changing? (Convicted/Challenged/ Changed)

_____

_____

_____

_____

_____

_____

_____

Date ___/___/___

Today I am a Child of God

Write a proclamation of belief. Each time you write, you are ensuring your vision and beliefs will carry on to the next generation.

_____

_____

_____

_____

_____

_____

_____

_____

_____

_____

How has my belief dictated my behavior today? (Faith)

_____

_____

_____

_____

_____

_____

How was I favored/How did I show favor? (Favor)

_____

_____

_____

_____

_____

_____

_____

What have I done to secure my future/What are My goals? (Future)

_____

_____

_____

_____

_____

_____

How have I stood firm in my walk and words? (Foundation/Walk/ Talk)

_____

_____

_____

_____

_____

_____

How have I displayed Christ's attitude/Where can I improve? (Attitude)

_____

_____

_____

_____

_____

_____

What Have I listened to that has stood out? (Hear)

_____

_____

_____

_____

_____

_____

What have I accomplished? (Do)

_____

_____

_____

_____

_____

_____

*How have I changed/am changing? (Convicted/Challenged/
Changed)*

_____

_____

_____

_____

_____

_____

Date ___/___/___

Today I am a Child of God

Write a proclamation of belief. Each time you write, you are ensuring your vision and beliefs will carry on to the next generation.

_____
_____
_____
_____
_____
_____
_____
_____
_____
_____

How has my belief dictated my behavior today? (Faith)

_____
_____
_____
_____
_____
_____
_____

How was I favored/How did I show favor? (Favor)

_____
_____
_____
_____

_____

_____

_____

What have I done to secure my future/What are My goals? (Future)

_____

_____

_____

_____

_____

_____

How have I stood firm in my walk and words? (Foundation/Walk/ Talk)

_____

_____

_____

_____

_____

How have I displayed Christ's attitude/Where can I improve? (Attitude)

_____

_____

_____

_____

_____
_____

What Have I listened to that has stood out? (Hear)

_____
_____
_____
_____
_____
_____
_____

What have I accomplished? (Do)

_____
_____
_____
_____
_____
_____

How have I changed/am changing? (Convicted/Challenged/ Changed)

_____
_____
_____
_____
_____
_____

Date ___/___/___

Today I am a Child of God

Write a proclamation of belief. Each time you write, you are ensuring your vision and beliefs will carry on to the next generation.

_____

_____

_____

_____

_____

_____

_____

_____

_____

How has my belief dictated my behavior today? (Faith)

_____

_____

_____

_____

_____

How was I favored/How did I show favor? (Favor)

_____

_____

_____

_____

_____

_____

What have I done to secure my future/What are My goals? (Future)

_____

_____

_____

_____

_____

_____

_____

How have I stood firm in my walk and words? (Foundation/Walk/ Talk)

_____

_____

_____

_____

_____

_____

_____

How have I displayed Christ's attitude/Where can I improve? (Attitude)

_____

_____

_____

_____

_____

_____
_____

What Have I listened to that has stood out? (Hear)

_____
_____
_____
_____
_____
_____
_____

What have I accomplished? (Do)

_____
_____
_____
_____
_____
_____
_____

How have I changed/am changing? (Convicted/Challenged/
Changed)

_____
_____
_____
_____
_____
_____
_____

Date ___/___/___

Today I am a Child of God

Write a proclamation of belief. Each time you write, you are ensuring your vision and beliefs will carry on to the next generation.

_____

_____

_____

_____

_____

_____

_____

_____

_____

How has my belief dictated my behavior today? (Faith)

_____

_____

_____

_____

_____

_____

How was I favored/How did I show favor? (Favor)

_____

_____

_____

_____

_____

_____

What have I done to secure my future/What are My goals? (Future)

_____

_____

_____

_____

_____

_____

_____

How have I stood firm in my walk and words? (Foundation/Walk/ Talk)

_____

_____

_____

_____

_____

_____

_____

How have I displayed Christ's attitude/Where can I improve? (Attitude)

_____

_____

_____

_____

_____

_____

_____

What Have I listened to that has stood out? (Hear)

_____

_____

_____

_____

_____

_____

What have I accomplished? (Do)

_____

_____

_____

_____

_____

_____

How have I changed/am changing? (Convicted/Challenged/ Changed)

_____

_____

_____

_____

_____

_____

Date ___/___/___

Today I am a Child of God

Write a proclamation of belief. Each time you write, you are ensuring your vision and beliefs will carry on to the next generation.

_____

_____

_____

_____

_____

_____

_____

_____

_____

_____

How has my belief dictated my behavior today? (Faith)

_____

_____

_____

_____

_____

_____

How was I favored/How did I show favor? (Favor)

_____

_____

_____

_____

_____

_____

_____

What have I done to secure my future/What are My goals?
(Future)

_____

_____

_____

_____

_____

_____

_____

How have I stood firm in my walk and words? (Foundation/Walk/
Talk)

_____

_____

_____

_____

_____

_____

_____

How have I displayed Christ's attitude/Where can I improve?
(Attitude)

_____

_____

_____

_____

_____

_____
_____

What Have I listened to that has stood out? (Hear)

_____
_____
_____
_____
_____
_____

What have I accomplished? (Do)

_____
_____
_____
_____
_____
_____

How have I changed/am changing? (Convicted/Challenged/Changed)

_____
_____
_____
_____
_____
_____

Date ___/___/___

Today I am a Child of God

Write a proclamation of belief. Each time you write, you are ensuring your vision and beliefs will carry on to the next generation.

_____
_____
_____
_____
_____
_____
_____
_____
_____
_____

How has my belief dictated my behavior today? (Faith)

_____
_____
_____
_____
_____
_____
_____

How was I favored/How did I show favor? (Favor)

_____
_____
_____
_____

_____

_____

_____

What have I done to secure my future/What are My goals? (Future)

_____

_____

_____

_____

_____

_____

_____

How have I stood firm in my walk and words? (Foundation/Walk/ Talk)

_____

_____

_____

_____

_____

_____

_____

How have I displayed Christ's attitude/Where can I improve? (Attitude)

_____

_____

_____

_____

_____

_____

_____

What Have I listened to that has stood out? (Hear)

_____

_____

_____

_____

_____

_____

_____

What have I accomplished? (Do)

_____

_____

_____

_____

_____

_____

_____

How have I changed/am changing? (Convicted/Challenged/Changed)

_____

_____

_____

_____

_____

_____

_____

Date ___/___/___

Today I am a Child of God

Write a proclamation of belief. Each time you write, you are ensuring your vision and beliefs will carry on to the next generation.

_____
_____
_____
_____
_____
_____
_____
_____
_____

How has my belief dictated my behavior today? (Faith)

_____
_____
_____
_____
_____
_____
_____

How was I favored/How did I show favor? (Favor)

_____
_____
_____
_____

_____

_____

_____

What have I done to secure my future/What are My goals? (Future)

_____

_____

_____

_____

_____

_____

_____

How have I stood firm in my walk and words? (Foundation/Walk/ Talk)

_____

_____

_____

_____

_____

_____

_____

How have I displayed Christ's attitude/Where can I improve? (Attitude)

_____

_____

_____

_____

_____

_____

_____

What Have I listened to that has stood out? (Hear)

_____

_____

_____

_____

_____

_____

What have I accomplished? (Do)

_____

_____

_____

_____

_____

_____

How have I changed/am changing? (Convicted/Challenged/ Changed)

_____

_____

_____

_____

_____

_____

Date ___/___/___

Today I am a Child of God

Write a proclamation of belief. Each time you write, you are ensuring your vision and beliefs will carry on to the next generation.

_____
_____
_____
_____
_____
_____
_____
_____
_____
_____

How has my belief dictated my behavior today? (Faith)

_____
_____
_____
_____
_____
_____

How was I favored/How did I show favor? (Favor)

_____
_____
_____
_____

_____

_____

_____

What have I done to secure my future/What are My goals? (Future)

_____

_____

_____

_____

_____

_____

_____

How have I stood firm in my walk and words? (Foundation/Walk/ Talk)

_____

_____

_____

_____

_____

_____

_____

How have I displayed Christ's attitude/Where can I improve? (Attitude)

_____

_____

_____

_____

_____

_____
_____

What Have I listened to that has stood out? (Hear)

_____
_____
_____
_____
_____
_____
_____

What have I accomplished? (Do)

_____
_____
_____
_____
_____
_____
_____

How have I changed/am changing? (Convicted/Challenged/ Changed)

_____
_____
_____
_____
_____
_____
_____

Date ___/___/___

Today I am a Child of God

Write a proclamation of belief. Each time you write, you are ensuring your vision and beliefs will carry on to the next generation.

_____

_____

_____

_____

_____

_____

_____

_____

_____

How has my belief dictated my behavior today? (Faith)

_____

_____

_____

_____

_____

_____

How was I favored/How did I show favor? (Favor)

_____

_____

_____

_____
_____
_____

What have I done to secure my future/What are My goals? (Future)

_____
_____
_____
_____
_____
_____
_____

How have I stood firm in my walk and words? (Foundation/Walk/ Talk)

_____
_____
_____
_____
_____
_____
_____

How have I displayed Christ's attitude/Where can I improve? (Attitude)

_____
_____
_____
_____
_____

_____
_____

What Have I listened to that has stood out? (Hear)

_____
_____
_____
_____
_____
_____
_____

What have I accomplished? (Do)

_____
_____
_____
_____
_____
_____
_____

How have I changed/am changing? (Convicted/Challenged/Changed)

_____
_____
_____
_____
_____
_____
_____

Date ___/___/___

Today I am a Child of God

Write a proclamation of belief. Each time you write, you are ensuring your vision and beliefs will carry on to the next generation.

_____
_____
_____
_____
_____
_____
_____
_____
_____
_____

How has my belief dictated my behavior today? (Faith)

_____
_____
_____
_____
_____
_____

How was I favored/How did I show favor? (Favor)

_____
_____
_____
_____

_____

_____

_____

What have I done to secure my future/What are My goals?
(Future)

_____

_____

_____

_____

_____

_____

_____

How have I stood firm in my walk and words? (Foundation/Walk/
Talk)

_____

_____

_____

_____

_____

_____

_____

How have I displayed Christ's attitude/Where can I improve?
(Attitude)

_____

_____

_____

_____

_____

_____
_____

What Have I listened to that has stood out? (Hear)

_____
_____
_____
_____
_____
_____
_____

What have I accomplished? (Do)

_____
_____
_____
_____
_____
_____

How have I changed/am changing? (Convicted/Challenged/ Changed)

_____
_____
_____
_____
_____
_____

Date ___/___/___

Today I am a Child of God

Write a proclamation of belief. Each time you write, you are ensuring your vision and beliefs will carry on to the next generation.

_____
_____
_____
_____
_____
_____
_____
_____
_____
_____

How has my belief dictated my behavior today? (Faith)

_____
_____
_____
_____
_____
_____

How was I favored/How did I show favor? (Favor)

_____
_____
_____
_____

_____

_____

_____

What have I done to secure my future/What are My goals? (Future)

_____

_____

_____

_____

_____

_____

_____

How have I stood firm in my walk and words? (Foundation/Walk/ Talk)

_____

_____

_____

_____

_____

_____

_____

How have I displayed Christ's attitude/Where can I improve? (Attitude)

_____

_____

_____

_____

_____

_____

_____

What Have I listened to that has stood out? (Hear)

_____

_____

_____

_____

_____

_____

What have I accomplished? (Do)

_____

_____

_____

_____

_____

_____

How have I changed/am changing? (Convicted/Challenged/ Changed)

_____

_____

_____

_____

_____

_____

Date ___/___/___

Today I am a Child of God

Write a proclamation of belief. Each time you write, you are ensuring your vision and beliefs will carry on to the next generation.

_____

_____

_____

_____

_____

_____

_____

_____

_____

_____

How has my belief dictated my behavior today? (Faith)

_____

_____

_____

_____

_____

_____

_____

How was I favored/How did I show favor? (Favor)

_____

_____

_____

_____

_____

_____

_____

What have I done to secure my future/What are My goals? (Future)

_____

_____

_____

_____

_____

_____

How have I stood firm in my walk and words? (Foundation/Walk/ Talk)

_____

_____

_____

_____

_____

_____

How have I displayed Christ's attitude/Where can I improve? (Attitude)

_____

_____

_____

_____

_____

_____
_____

What Have I listened to that has stood out? (Hear)

_____
_____
_____
_____
_____
_____
_____

What have I accomplished? (Do)

_____
_____
_____
_____
_____
_____
_____

How have I changed/am changing? (Convicted/Challenged/Changed)

_____
_____
_____
_____
_____
_____
_____

Date ___/___/___

Today I am a Child of God

Write a proclamation of belief. Each time you write, you are ensuring your vision and beliefs will carry on to the next generation.

_____

_____

_____

_____

_____

_____

_____

_____

_____

_____

How has my belief dictated my behavior today? (Faith)

_____

_____

_____

_____

_____

_____

How was I favored/How did I show favor? (Favor)

_____

_____

_____

_____

_____

_____

_____

*What have I done to secure my future/What are My goals?
(Future)*

_____

_____

_____

_____

_____

_____

_____

*How have I stood firm in my walk and words? (Foundation/Walk/
Talk)*

_____

_____

_____

_____

_____

_____

_____

*How have I displayed Christ's attitude/Where can I improve?
(Attitude)*

_____

_____

_____

_____

_____

_____

_____

What Have I listened to that has stood out? (Hear)

_____

_____

_____

_____

_____

_____

What have I accomplished? (Do)

_____

_____

_____

_____

_____

_____

How have I changed/am changing? (Convicted/Challenged/Changed)

_____

_____

_____

_____

_____

_____

Date ___/___/___

Today I am a Child of God

Write a proclamation of belief. Each time you write, you are ensuring your vision and beliefs will carry on to the next generation.

_____
_____
_____
_____
_____
_____
_____
_____
_____

How has my belief dictated my behavior today? (Faith)

_____
_____
_____
_____
_____
_____

How was I favored/How did I show favor? (Favor)

_____
_____
_____
_____

_____

_____

_____

*What have I done to secure my future/What are My goals?
(Future)*

_____

_____

_____

_____

_____

_____

_____

*How have I stood firm in my walk and words? (Foundation/Walk/
Talk)*

_____

_____

_____

_____

_____

_____

_____

*How have I displayed Christ's attitude/Where can I improve?
(Attitude)*

_____

_____

_____

_____

_____

_____

_____

What Have I listened to that has stood out? (Hear)

_____

_____

_____

_____

_____

_____

_____

What have I accomplished? (Do)

_____

_____

_____

_____

_____

_____

_____

How have I changed/am changing? (Convicted/Challenged/ Changed)

_____

_____

_____

_____

_____

_____

_____

Date ___/___/___

Today I am a Child of God

Write a proclamation of belief. Each time you write, you are ensuring your vision and beliefs will carry on to the next generation.

_____

_____

_____

_____

_____

_____

_____

_____

_____

How has my belief dictated my behavior today? (Faith)

_____

_____

_____

_____

_____

_____

How was I favored/How did I show favor? (Favor)

_____

_____

_____

_____

_____
_____
_____

What have I done to secure my future/What are My goals? (Future)

_____
_____
_____
_____
_____
_____
_____

How have I stood firm in my walk and words? (Foundation/Walk/ Talk)

_____
_____
_____
_____
_____
_____
_____

How have I displayed Christ's attitude/Where can I improve? (Attitude)

_____
_____
_____
_____
_____

_____
_____

What Have I listened to that has stood out? (Hear)

_____
_____
_____
_____
_____
_____

What have I accomplished? (Do)

_____
_____
_____
_____
_____
_____

How have I changed/am changing? (Convicted/Challenged/Changed)

_____
_____
_____
_____
_____
_____

Date ___/___/___

Today I am a Child of God

Write a proclamation of belief. Each time you write, you are ensuring your vision and beliefs will carry on to the next generation.

_____
_____
_____
_____
_____
_____
_____
_____
_____
_____

How has my belief dictated my behavior today? (Faith)

_____
_____
_____
_____
_____
_____

How was I favored/How did I show favor? (Favor)

_____
_____
_____
_____

_____

_____

_____

What have I done to secure my future/What are My goals? (Future)

_____

_____

_____

_____

_____

_____

_____

How have I stood firm in my walk and words? (Foundation/Walk/ Talk)

_____

_____

_____

_____

_____

_____

How have I displayed Christ's attitude/Where can I improve? (Attitude)

_____

_____

_____

_____

_____

_____
_____

What Have I listened to that has stood out? (Hear)

_____
_____
_____
_____
_____
_____
_____

What have I accomplished? (Do)

_____
_____
_____
_____
_____
_____
_____

*How have I changed/am changing? (Convicted/Challenged/
Changed)*

_____
_____
_____
_____
_____
_____
_____

Date ___/___/___

Today I am a Child of God

Write a proclamation of belief. Each time you write, you are ensuring your vision and beliefs will carry on to the next generation.

_____

_____

_____

_____

_____

_____

_____

_____

_____

_____

How has my belief dictated my behavior today? (Faith)

_____

_____

_____

_____

_____

_____

_____

How was I favored/How did I show favor? (Favor)

_____

_____

_____

_____

_____

_____

_____

What have I done to secure my future/What are My goals? (Future)

_____

_____

_____

_____

_____

_____

How have I stood firm in my walk and words? (Foundation/Walk/ Talk)

_____

_____

_____

_____

_____

_____

How have I displayed Christ's attitude/Where can I improve? (Attitude)

_____

_____

_____

_____

What Have I listened to that has stood out? (Hear)

_____

_____

_____

_____

_____

_____

What have I accomplished? (Do)

_____

_____

_____

_____

_____

_____

How have I changed/am changing? (Convicted/Challenged/Changed)

_____

_____

_____

_____

_____

_____

Date ___/___/___

Today I am a Child of God

Write a proclamation of belief. Each time you write, you are ensuring your vision and beliefs will carry on to the next generation.

_____
_____
_____
_____
_____
_____
_____
_____
_____
_____

How has my belief dictated my behavior today? (Faith)

_____
_____
_____
_____
_____
_____
_____

How was I favored/How did I show favor? (Favor)

_____
_____
_____
_____

_____

_____

_____

What have I done to secure my future/What are My goals? (Future)

_____

_____

_____

_____

_____

_____

How have I stood firm in my walk and words? (Foundation/Walk/ Talk)

_____

_____

_____

_____

_____

_____

How have I displayed Christ's attitude/Where can I improve? (Attitude)

_____

_____

_____

_____

_____

_____
_____

What Have I listened to that has stood out? (Hear)

_____
_____
_____
_____
_____
_____
_____

What have I accomplished? (Do)

_____
_____
_____
_____
_____
_____
_____

How have I changed/am changing? (Convicted/Challenged/Changed)

_____
_____
_____
_____
_____
_____
_____

Date ___/___/___

Today I am a Child of God

Write a proclamation of belief. Each time you write, you are ensuring your vision and beliefs will carry on to the next generation.

_____

_____

_____

_____

_____

_____

_____

_____

_____

_____

How has my belief dictated my behavior today? (Faith)

_____

_____

_____

_____

_____

_____

How was I favored/How did I show favor? (Favor)

_____

_____

_____

_____

_____

_____

_____

What have I done to secure my future/What are My goals? (Future)

_____

_____

_____

_____

_____

_____

_____

How have I stood firm in my walk and words? (Foundation/Walk/ Talk)

_____

_____

_____

_____

_____

_____

_____

How have I displayed Christ's attitude/Where can I improve? (Attitude)

_____

_____

_____

_____

_____

_____

What Have I listened to that has stood out? (Hear)

_____

_____

_____

_____

_____

_____

What have I accomplished? (Do)

_____

_____

_____

_____

_____

_____

How have I changed/am changing? (Convicted/Challenged/ Changed)

_____

_____

_____

_____

_____

_____

_____

Date ___/___/___

Today I am a Child of God

Write a proclamation of belief. Each time you write, you are ensuring your vision and beliefs will carry on to the next generation.

_____

_____

_____

_____

_____

_____

_____

_____

_____

_____

How has my belief dictated my behavior today? (Faith)

_____

_____

_____

_____

_____

_____

How was I favored/How did I show favor? (Favor)

_____

_____

_____

_____

_____

_____

What have I done to secure my future/What are My goals? (Future)

_____

_____

_____

_____

_____

_____

How have I stood firm in my walk and words? (Foundation/Walk/ Talk)

_____

_____

_____

_____

_____

_____

How have I displayed Christ's attitude/Where can I improve? (Attitude)

_____

_____

_____

_____

_____

_____

_____

What Have I listened to that has stood out? (Hear)

_____

_____

_____

_____

_____

_____

_____

What have I accomplished? (Do)

_____

_____

_____

_____

_____

_____

How have I changed/am changing? (Convicted/Challenged/ Changed)

_____

_____

_____

_____

_____

_____

Date ___/___/___

Today I am a Child of God

Write a proclamation of belief. Each time you write, you are ensuring your vision and beliefs will carry on to the next generation.

_____

_____

_____

_____

_____

_____

_____

_____

_____

_____

How has my belief dictated my behavior today? (Faith)

_____

_____

_____

_____

_____

_____

How was I favored/How did I show favor? (Favor)

_____

_____

_____

_____

_____

_____

_____

What have I done to secure my future/What are My goals?
(Future)

_____

_____

_____

_____

_____

_____

_____

How have I stood firm in my walk and words? (Foundation/Walk/
Talk)

_____

_____

_____

_____

_____

_____

_____

How have I displayed Christ's attitude/Where can I improve?
(Attitude)

_____

_____

_____

_____

_____

_____

_____

What Have I listened to that has stood out? (Hear)

_____

_____

_____

_____

_____

_____

What have I accomplished? (Do)

_____

_____

_____

_____

_____

_____

How have I changed/am changing? (Convicted/Challenged/Changed)

_____

_____

_____

_____

_____

_____

Date ___/___/___

Today I am a Child of God

Write a proclamation of belief. Each time you write, you are ensuring your vision and beliefs will carry on to the next generation.

_____
_____
_____
_____
_____
_____
_____
_____
_____
_____

How has my belief dictated my behavior today? (Faith)

_____
_____
_____
_____
_____
_____

How was I favored/How did I show favor? (Favor)

_____
_____
_____
_____

_____
_____
_____
_____

What have I done to secure my future/What are My goals? (Future)

_____
_____
_____
_____
_____
_____
_____

How have I stood firm in my walk and words? (Foundation/Walk/ Talk)

_____
_____
_____
_____
_____
_____
_____

How have I displayed Christ's attitude/Where can I improve? (Attitude)

_____
_____
_____
_____
_____

_____

_____

What Have I listened to that has stood out? (Hear)

_____

_____

_____

_____

_____

_____

_____

What have I accomplished? (Do)

_____

_____

_____

_____

_____

_____

_____

How have I changed/am changing? (Convicted/Challenged/ Changed)

_____

_____

_____

_____

_____

_____

_____

Date ___/___/___

Today I am a Child of God

Write a proclamation of belief. Each time you write, you are ensuring your vision and beliefs will carry on to the next generation.

_____
_____
_____
_____
_____
_____
_____
_____
_____

How has my belief dictated my behavior today? (Faith)

_____
_____
_____
_____
_____
_____

How was I favored/How did I show favor? (Favor)

_____
_____
_____
_____

_____
_____
_____

What have I done to secure my future/What are My goals? (Future)

_____
_____
_____
_____
_____
_____
_____

How have I stood firm in my walk and words? (Foundation/Walk/ Talk)

_____
_____
_____
_____
_____
_____

How have I displayed Christ's attitude/Where can I improve? (Attitude)

_____
_____
_____
_____

_____

_____

What Have I listened to that has stood out? (Hear)

_____

_____

_____

_____

_____

_____

What have I accomplished? (Do)

_____

_____

_____

_____

_____

_____

How have I changed/am changing? (Convicted/Challenged/ Changed)

_____

_____

_____

_____

_____

_____

Date ___/___/___

Today I am a Child of God

Write a proclamation of belief. Each time you write, you are ensuring your vision and beliefs will carry on to the next generation.

_____
_____
_____
_____
_____
_____
_____
_____
_____
_____

How has my belief dictated my behavior today? (Faith)

_____
_____
_____
_____
_____
_____

How was I favored/How did I show favor? (Favor)

_____
_____
_____
_____

_____

_____

_____

What have I done to secure my future/What are My goals? (Future)

_____

_____

_____

_____

_____

_____

_____

How have I stood firm in my walk and words? (Foundation/Walk/ Talk)

_____

_____

_____

_____

_____

_____

_____

How have I displayed Christ's attitude/Where can I improve? (Attitude)

_____

_____

_____

_____

_____

_____

_____

What Have I listened to that has stood out? (Hear)

_____

_____

_____

_____

_____

_____

What have I accomplished? (Do)

_____

_____

_____

_____

_____

_____

How have I changed/am changing? (Convicted/Challenged/ Changed)

_____

_____

_____

_____

_____

_____

Date ___/___/___

Today I am a Child of God

Write a proclamation of belief. Each time you write, you are ensuring your vision and beliefs will carry on to the next generation.

_____

_____

_____

_____

_____

_____

_____

_____

_____

_____

How has my belief dictated my behavior today? (Faith)

_____

_____

_____

_____

_____

_____

_____

How was I favored/How did I show favor? (Favor)

_____

_____

_____

_____

_____

_____

_____

What have I done to secure my future/What are My goals? (Future)

_____

_____

_____

_____

_____

_____

How have I stood firm in my walk and words? (Foundation/Walk/ Talk)

_____

_____

_____

_____

_____

_____

_____

How have I displayed Christ's attitude/Where can I improve? (Attitude)

_____

_____

_____

_____

_____

_____

_____

What Have I listened to that has stood out? (Hear)

_____

_____

_____

_____

_____

_____

_____

What have I accomplished? (Do)

_____

_____

_____

_____

_____

_____

_____

*How have I changed/am changing? (Convicted/Challenged/
Changed)*

_____

_____

_____

_____

_____

_____

_____

Date ___/___/___

Today I am a Child of God

Write a proclamation of belief. Each time you write, you are ensuring your vision and beliefs will carry on to the next generation.

_____
_____
_____
_____
_____
_____
_____
_____
_____
_____

How has my belief dictated my behavior today? (Faith)

_____
_____
_____
_____
_____
_____

How was I favored/How did I show favor? (Favor)

_____
_____
_____
_____

_____

_____

_____

What have I done to secure my future/What are My goals? (Future)

_____

_____

_____

_____

_____

_____

_____

How have I stood firm in my walk and words? (Foundation/Walk/ Talk)

_____

_____

_____

_____

_____

_____

How have I displayed Christ's attitude/Where can I improve? (Attitude)

_____

_____

_____

_____

_____

_____
_____

What Have I listened to that has stood out? (Hear)

_____
_____
_____
_____
_____
_____

What have I accomplished? (Do)

_____
_____
_____
_____
_____
_____

How have I changed/am changing? (Convicted/Challenged/Changed)

_____
_____
_____
_____
_____
_____

Date ___/___/___

Today I am a Child of God

Write a proclamation of belief. Each time you write, you are ensuring your vision and beliefs will carry on to the next generation.

_____
_____
_____
_____
_____
_____
_____
_____
_____

How has my belief dictated my behavior today? (Faith)

_____
_____
_____
_____
_____
_____

How was I favored/How did I show favor? (Favor)

_____
_____
_____
_____

_____
_____
_____

What have I done to secure my future/What are My goals? (Future)

_____
_____
_____
_____
_____
_____
_____

How have I stood firm in my walk and words? (Foundation/Walk/ Talk)

_____
_____
_____
_____
_____
_____
_____

How have I displayed Christ's attitude/Where can I improve? (Attitude)

_____
_____
_____
_____
_____

_____
_____

What Have I listened to that has stood out? (Hear)

_____
_____
_____
_____
_____
_____

What have I accomplished? (Do)

_____
_____
_____
_____
_____
_____

How have I changed/am changing? (Convicted/Challenged/ Changed)

_____
_____
_____
_____
_____
_____

Date ___/___/___

Today I am a Child of God

Write a proclamation of belief. Each time you write, you are ensuring your vision and beliefs will carry on to the next generation.

_____
_____
_____
_____
_____
_____
_____
_____
_____

How has my belief dictated my behavior today? (Faith)

_____
_____
_____
_____
_____
_____

How was I favored/How did I show favor? (Favor)

_____
_____
_____
_____

_____
_____
_____

What have I done to secure my future/What are My goals? (Future)

_____
_____
_____
_____
_____
_____
_____

How have I stood firm in my walk and words? (Foundation/Walk/ Talk)

_____
_____
_____
_____
_____
_____
_____

How have I displayed Christ's attitude/Where can I improve? (Attitude)

_____
_____
_____
_____
_____

_____

_____

What Have I listened to that has stood out? (Hear)

_____

_____

_____

_____

_____

_____

_____

What have I accomplished? (Do)

_____

_____

_____

_____

_____

_____

_____

How have I changed/am changing? (Convicted/Challenged/Changed)

_____

_____

_____

_____

_____

_____

_____

Date ___/___/___

Today I am a Child of God

Write a proclamation of belief. Each time you write, you are ensuring your vision and beliefs will carry on to the next generation.

_____
_____
_____
_____
_____
_____
_____
_____
_____
_____

How has my belief dictated my behavior today? (Faith)

_____
_____
_____
_____
_____
_____

How was I favored/How did I show favor? (Favor)

_____
_____
_____
_____

_____

_____

_____

What have I done to secure my future/What are My goals? (Future)

_____

_____

_____

_____

_____

_____

How have I stood firm in my walk and words? (Foundation/Walk/ Talk)

_____

_____

_____

_____

_____

_____

How have I displayed Christ's attitude/Where can I improve? (Attitude)

_____

_____

_____

_____

_____

_____

What Have I listened to that has stood out? (Hear)

_____

_____

_____

_____

_____

_____

_____

What have I accomplished? (Do)

_____

_____

_____

_____

_____

_____

_____

How have I changed/am changing? (Convicted/Challenged/Changed)

_____

_____

_____

_____

_____

_____

_____

Date ___/___/___

Today I am a Child of God

Write a proclamation of belief. Each time you write, you are ensuring your vision and beliefs will carry on to the next generation.

_____
_____
_____
_____
_____
_____
_____
_____
_____
_____

How has my belief dictated my behavior today? (Faith)

_____
_____
_____
_____
_____
_____
_____

How was I favored/How did I show favor? (Favor)

_____
_____
_____
_____

_____
_____
_____

What have I done to secure my future/What are My goals? (Future)

_____
_____
_____
_____
_____
_____
_____

How have I stood firm in my walk and words? (Foundation/Walk/ Talk)

_____
_____
_____
_____
_____
_____

How have I displayed Christ's attitude/Where can I improve? (Attitude)

_____
_____
_____
_____

_____
_____

What Have I listened to that has stood out? (Hear)

_____
_____
_____
_____
_____
_____
_____

What have I accomplished? (Do)

_____
_____
_____
_____
_____
_____
_____

How have I changed/am changing? (Convicted/Challenged/
Changed)

_____
_____
_____
_____
_____
_____
_____

Date ___/___/___

Today I am a Child of God

Write a proclamation of belief. Each time you write, you are ensuring your vision and beliefs will carry on to the next generation.

_____
_____
_____
_____
_____
_____
_____
_____
_____
_____

How has my belief dictated my behavior today? (Faith)

_____
_____
_____
_____
_____
_____
_____

How was I favored/How did I show favor? (Favor)

_____
_____
_____
_____

_____

_____

_____

What have I done to secure my future/What are My goals?
(Future)

_____

_____

_____

_____

_____

_____

How have I stood firm in my walk and words? (Foundation/Walk/
Talk)

_____

_____

_____

_____

_____

_____

How have I displayed Christ's attitude/Where can I improve?
(Attitude)

_____

_____

_____

_____

_____

What Have I listened to that has stood out? (Hear)

_____
_____
_____
_____
_____
_____
_____

What have I accomplished? (Do)

_____
_____
_____
_____
_____
_____
_____

How have I changed/am changing? (Convicted/Challenged/ Changed)

_____
_____
_____
_____
_____
_____
_____

Date ___/___/___

Today I am a Child of God

Write a proclamation of belief. Each time you write, you are ensuring your vision and beliefs will carry on to the next generation.

_____
_____
_____
_____
_____
_____
_____
_____
_____
_____

How has my belief dictated my behavior today? (Faith)

_____
_____
_____
_____
_____
_____

How was I favored/How did I show favor? (Favor)

_____
_____
_____
_____

_____
_____
_____

What have I done to secure my future/What are My goals? (Future)

_____
_____
_____
_____
_____
_____
_____

How have I stood firm in my walk and words? (Foundation/Walk/ Talk)

_____
_____
_____
_____
_____
_____
_____

How have I displayed Christ's attitude/Where can I improve? (Attitude)

_____
_____
_____
_____
_____

_____

_____

What Have I listened to that has stood out? (Hear)

_____

_____

_____

_____

_____

_____

_____

What have I accomplished? (Do)

_____

_____

_____

_____

_____

_____

How have I changed/am changing? (Convicted/Challenged/ Changed)

_____

_____

_____

_____

_____

_____

Date ___/___/___

Today I am a Child of God

Write a proclamation of belief. Each time you write, you are ensuring your vision and beliefs will carry on to the next generation.

_____

_____

_____

_____

_____

_____

_____

_____

_____

_____

How has my belief dictated my behavior today? (Faith)

_____

_____

_____

_____

_____

_____

How was I favored/How did I show favor? (Favor)

_____

_____

_____

_____

_____

_____

_____

What have I done to secure my future/What are My goals? (Future)

_____

_____

_____

_____

_____

_____

_____

How have I stood firm in my walk and words? (Foundation/Walk/Talk)

_____

_____

_____

_____

_____

_____

_____

How have I displayed Christ's attitude/Where can I improve? (Attitude)

_____

_____

_____

_____

_____

_____

_____

What Have I listened to that has stood out? (Hear)

_____

_____

_____

_____

_____

_____

What have I accomplished? (Do)

_____

_____

_____

_____

_____

_____

How have I changed/am changing? (Convicted/Challenged/ Changed)

_____

_____

_____

_____

_____

_____

Date ___/___/___

Today I am a Child of God

Write a proclamation of belief. Each time you write, you are ensuring your vision and beliefs will carry on to the next generation.

_____
_____
_____
_____
_____
_____
_____
_____
_____
_____
_____

How has my belief dictated my behavior today? (Faith)

_____
_____
_____
_____
_____
_____
_____

How was I favored/How did I show favor? (Favor)

_____
_____
_____
_____

_____

_____

_____

What have I done to secure my future/What are My goals? (Future)

_____

_____

_____

_____

_____

_____

_____

How have I stood firm in my walk and words? (Foundation/Walk/ Talk)

_____

_____

_____

_____

_____

_____

_____

How have I displayed Christ's attitude/Where can I improve? (Attitude)

_____

_____

_____

_____

_____

_____
_____

What Have I listened to that has stood out? (Hear)

_____
_____
_____
_____
_____
_____

What have I accomplished? (Do)

_____
_____
_____
_____
_____
_____

How have I changed/am changing? (Convicted/Challenged/Changed)

_____
_____
_____
_____
_____
_____

Date ___/___/___

Today I am a Child of God

Write a proclamation of belief. Each time you write, you are ensuring your vision and beliefs will carry on to the next generation.

_____

_____

_____

_____

_____

_____

_____

_____

_____

_____

How has my belief dictated my behavior today? (Faith)

_____

_____

_____

_____

_____

How was I favored/How did I show favor? (Favor)

_____

_____

_____

_____

_____

_____

What have I done to secure my future/What are My goals? (Future)

_____

_____

_____

_____

_____

_____

How have I stood firm in my walk and words? (Foundation/Walk/ Talk)

_____

_____

_____

_____

_____

_____

How have I displayed Christ's attitude/Where can I improve? (Attitude)

_____

_____

_____

_____

_____

_____
_____

What Have I listened to that has stood out? (Hear)

_____
_____
_____
_____
_____
_____

What have I accomplished? (Do)

_____
_____
_____
_____
_____
_____

How have I changed/am changing? (Convicted/Challenged/ Changed)

_____
_____
_____
_____
_____
_____

Date ___/___/___

Today I am a Child of God

Write a proclamation of belief. Each time you write, you are ensuring your vision and beliefs will carry on to the next generation.

_____
_____
_____
_____
_____
_____
_____
_____
_____
_____

How has my belief dictated my behavior today? (Faith)

_____
_____
_____
_____
_____
_____

How was I favored/How did I show favor? (Favor)

_____
_____
_____
_____

_____

_____

_____

What have I done to secure my future/What are My goals? (Future)

_____

_____

_____

_____

_____

_____

How have I stood firm in my walk and words? (Foundation/Walk/ Talk)

_____

_____

_____

_____

_____

_____

How have I displayed Christ's attitude/Where can I improve? (Attitude)

_____

_____

_____

_____

_____

_____

_____

What Have I listened to that has stood out? (Hear)

_____

_____

_____

_____

_____

_____

_____

What have I accomplished? (Do)

_____

_____

_____

_____

_____

_____

How have I changed/am changing? (Convicted/Challenged/Changed)

_____

_____

_____

_____

_____

_____

Date ___/___/___

Today I am a Child of God

Write a proclamation of belief. Each time you write, you are ensuring your vision and beliefs will carry on to the next generation.

_____
_____
_____
_____
_____
_____
_____
_____
_____

How has my belief dictated my behavior today? (Faith)

_____
_____
_____
_____
_____
_____
_____

How was I favored/How did I show favor? (Favor)

_____
_____
_____
_____

_____

_____

_____

What have I done to secure my future/What are My goals?
(Future)

_____

_____

_____

_____

_____

_____

_____

How have I stood firm in my walk and words? (Foundation/Walk/
Talk)

_____

_____

_____

_____

_____

_____

_____

How have I displayed Christ's attitude/Where can I improve?
(Attitude)

_____

_____

_____

_____

_____

_____

_____

What Have I listened to that has stood out? (Hear)

_____

_____

_____

_____

_____

_____

What have I accomplished? (Do)

_____

_____

_____

_____

_____

_____

How have I changed/am changing? (Convicted/Challenged/Changed)

_____

_____

_____

_____

_____

_____

Date ___/___/___

Today I am a Child of God

Write a proclamation of belief. Each time you write, you are ensuring your vision and beliefs will carry on to the next generation.

_____
_____
_____
_____
_____
_____
_____
_____
_____
_____

How has my belief dictated my behavior today? (Faith)

_____
_____
_____
_____
_____
_____

How was I favored/How did I show favor? (Favor)

_____
_____
_____
_____

_____

_____

_____

What have I done to secure my future/What are My goals? (Future)

_____

_____

_____

_____

_____

_____

_____

How have I stood firm in my walk and words? (Foundation/Walk/ Talk)

_____

_____

_____

_____

_____

_____

How have I displayed Christ's attitude/Where can I improve? (Attitude)

_____

_____

_____

_____

_____

_____

_____

What Have I listened to that has stood out? (Hear)

_____

_____

_____

_____

_____

_____

What have I accomplished? (Do)

_____

_____

_____

_____

_____

_____

How have I changed/am changing? (Convicted/Challenged/ Changed)

_____

_____

_____

_____

_____

_____

Date ___/___/___

Today I am a Child of God

Write a proclamation of belief. Each time you write, you are ensuring your vision and beliefs will carry on to the next generation.

_____
_____
_____
_____
_____
_____
_____
_____
_____
_____

How has my belief dictated my behavior today? (Faith)

_____
_____
_____
_____
_____
_____

How was I favored/How did I show favor? (Favor)

_____
_____
_____
_____

_____

_____

_____

What have I done to secure my future/What are My goals? (Future)

_____

_____

_____

_____

_____

_____

_____

How have I stood firm in my walk and words? (Foundation/Walk/Talk)

_____

_____

_____

_____

_____

_____

_____

How have I displayed Christ's attitude/Where can I improve? (Attitude)

_____

_____

_____

_____

_____

_____

_____

What Have I listened to that has stood out? (Hear)

_____

_____

_____

_____

_____

_____

What have I accomplished? (Do)

_____

_____

_____

_____

_____

_____

How have I changed/am changing? (Convicted/Challenged/ Changed)

_____

_____

_____

_____

_____

_____

Date ___/___/___

Today I am a Child of God

Write a proclamation of belief. Each time you write, you are ensuring your vision and beliefs will carry on to the next generation.

_____
_____
_____
_____
_____
_____
_____
_____
_____
_____

How has my belief dictated my behavior today? (Faith)

_____
_____
_____
_____
_____
_____
_____

How was I favored/How did I show favor? (Favor)

_____
_____
_____

_____
_____
_____

What have I done to secure my future/What are My goals? (Future)

_____
_____
_____
_____
_____
_____
_____

How have I stood firm in my walk and words? (Foundation/Walk/ Talk)

_____
_____
_____
_____
_____
_____
_____

How have I displayed Christ's attitude/Where can I improve? (Attitude)

_____
_____
_____
_____
_____

_____
_____

What Have I listened to that has stood out? (Hear)

_____
_____
_____
_____
_____
_____
_____

What have I accomplished? (Do)

_____
_____
_____
_____
_____
_____
_____

How have I changed/am changing? (Convicted/Challenged/ Changed)

_____
_____
_____
_____
_____
_____
_____

Date ___/___/___

Today I am a Child of God

Write a proclamation of belief. Each time you write, you are ensuring your vision and beliefs will carry on to the next generation.

_____

_____

_____

_____

_____

_____

_____

_____

_____

How has my belief dictated my behavior today? (Faith)

_____

_____

_____

_____

_____

_____

How was I favored/How did I show favor? (Favor)

_____

_____

_____

_____

_____

_____

What have I done to secure my future/What are My goals? (Future)

_____

_____

_____

_____

_____

_____

_____

How have I stood firm in my walk and words? (Foundation/Walk/ Talk)

_____

_____

_____

_____

_____

_____

_____

How have I displayed Christ's attitude/Where can I improve? (Attitude)

_____

_____

_____

_____

_____

_____

What Have I listened to that has stood out? *(Hear)*

_____

_____

_____

_____

_____

_____

_____

What have I accomplished? *(Do)*

_____

_____

_____

_____

_____

_____

_____

How have I changed/am changing? *(Convicted/Challenged/Changed)*

_____

_____

_____

_____

_____

_____

_____

Date ___/___/___

Today I am a Child of God

Write a proclamation of belief. Each time you write, you are ensuring your vision and beliefs will carry on to the next generation.

_____
_____
_____
_____
_____
_____
_____
_____
_____
_____

How has my belief dictated my behavior today? (Faith)

_____
_____
_____
_____
_____
_____

How was I favored/How did I show favor? (Favor)

_____
_____
_____

_____

_____

_____

What have I done to secure my future/What are My goals? (Future)

_____

_____

_____

_____

_____

_____

_____

How have I stood firm in my walk and words? (Foundation/Walk/ Talk)

_____

_____

_____

_____

_____

_____

_____

How have I displayed Christ's attitude/Where can I improve? (Attitude)

_____

_____

_____

_____

_____

_____

_____

What Have I listened to that has stood out? (Hear)

_____

_____

_____

_____

_____

_____

What have I accomplished? (Do)

_____

_____

_____

_____

_____

_____

How have I changed/am changing? (Convicted/Challenged/Changed)

_____

_____

_____

_____

_____

_____

Date ___/___/___

Today I am a Child of God

Write a proclamation of belief. Each time you write, you are ensuring your vision and beliefs will carry on to the next generation.

_____
_____
_____
_____
_____
_____
_____
_____
_____

How has my belief dictated my behavior today? (Faith)

_____
_____
_____
_____
_____
_____
_____

How was I favored/How did I show favor? (Favor)

_____
_____
_____
_____

_____

_____

_____

What have I done to secure my future/What are My goals?
(Future)

_____

_____

_____

_____

_____

_____

_____

How have I stood firm in my walk and words? (Foundation/Walk/
Talk)

_____

_____

_____

_____

_____

_____

_____

How have I displayed Christ's attitude/Where can I improve?
(Attitude)

_____

_____

_____

_____

_____

_____
_____

What Have I listened to that has stood out? (Hear)

_____
_____
_____
_____
_____
_____

What have I accomplished? (Do)

_____
_____
_____
_____
_____
_____

*How have I changed/am changing? (Convicted/Challenged/
Changed)*

_____
_____
_____
_____
_____
_____

Date ___/___/___

Today I am a Child of God

Write a proclamation of belief. Each time you write, you are ensuring your vision and beliefs will carry on to the next generation.

_____
_____
_____
_____
_____
_____
_____
_____
_____

How has my belief dictated my behavior today? (Faith)

_____
_____
_____
_____
_____
_____

How was I favored/How did I show favor? (Favor)

_____
_____
_____
_____

_____
_____
_____
_____

What have I done to secure my future/What are My goals?
(Future)

_____
_____
_____
_____
_____
_____
_____

How have I stood firm in my walk and words? (Foundation/Walk/
Talk)

_____
_____
_____
_____
_____
_____

How have I displayed Christ's attitude/Where can I improve?
(Attitude)

_____
_____
_____
_____
_____

_____
_____

What Have I listened to that has stood out? (Hear)

_____
_____
_____
_____
_____
_____
_____

What have I accomplished? (Do)

_____
_____
_____
_____
_____
_____

How have I changed/am changing? (Convicted/Challenged/ Changed)

_____
_____
_____
_____
_____
_____

Date ___/___/___

Today I am a Child of God

Write a proclamation of belief. Each time you write, you are ensuring your vision and beliefs will carry on to the next generation.

_____
_____
_____
_____
_____
_____
_____
_____
_____
_____

How has my belief dictated my behavior today? (Faith)

_____
_____
_____
_____
_____
_____
_____

How was I favored/How did I show favor? (Favor)

_____
_____
_____
_____

_____
_____
_____

What have I done to secure my future/What are My goals?
(Future)

_____
_____
_____
_____
_____
_____
_____

How have I stood firm in my walk and words? (Foundation/Walk/
Talk)

_____
_____
_____
_____
_____
_____
_____

How have I displayed Christ's attitude/Where can I improve?
(Attitude)

_____
_____
_____
_____
_____

_____

_____

What Have I listened to that has stood out? (Hear)

_____

_____

_____

_____

_____

_____

_____

What have I accomplished? (Do)

_____

_____

_____

_____

_____

_____

_____

How have I changed/am changing? (Convicted/Challenged/ Changed)

_____

_____

_____

_____

_____

_____

_____

Date ___/___/___

Today I am a Child of God

Write a proclamation of belief. Each time you write, you are ensuring your vision and beliefs will carry on to the next generation.

_____
_____
_____
_____
_____
_____
_____
_____
_____

How has my belief dictated my behavior today? (Faith)

_____
_____
_____
_____
_____
_____

How was I favored/How did I show favor? (Favor)

_____
_____
_____
_____

_____

_____

_____

What have I done to secure my future/What are My goals?
(Future)

_____

_____

_____

_____

_____

_____

How have I stood firm in my walk and words? (Foundation/Walk/
Talk)

_____

_____

_____

_____

_____

_____

How have I displayed Christ's attitude/Where can I improve?
(Attitude)

_____

_____

_____

_____

_____
_____

What Have I listened to that has stood out? (Hear)

_____
_____
_____
_____
_____
_____
_____

What have I accomplished? (Do)

_____
_____
_____
_____
_____
_____
_____

How have I changed/am changing? (Convicted/Challenged/Changed)

_____
_____
_____
_____
_____
_____
_____

Date ___/___/___

Today I am a Child of God

Write a proclamation of belief. Each time you write, you are ensuring your vision and beliefs will carry on to the next generation.

_____

_____

_____

_____

_____

_____

_____

_____

_____

How has my belief dictated my behavior today? (Faith)

_____

_____

_____

_____

_____

_____

How was I favored/How did I show favor? (Favor)

_____

_____

_____

_____

_____

_____

What have I done to secure my future/What are My goals? (Future)

_____

_____

_____

_____

_____

_____

_____

How have I stood firm in my walk and words? (Foundation/Walk/ Talk)

_____

_____

_____

_____

_____

_____

_____

How have I displayed Christ's attitude/Where can I improve? (Attitude)

_____

_____

_____

_____

_____

_____

_____

What Have I listened to that has stood out? (Hear)

_____

_____

_____

_____

_____

_____

What have I accomplished? (Do)

_____

_____

_____

_____

_____

_____

How have I changed/am changing? (Convicted/Challenged/Changed)

_____

_____

_____

_____

_____

_____

Date ___/___/___

Today I am a Child of God

Write a proclamation of belief. Each time you write, you are ensuring your vision and beliefs will carry on to the next generation.

_____
_____
_____
_____
_____
_____
_____
_____
_____
_____

How has my belief dictated my behavior today? (Faith)

_____
_____
_____
_____
_____
_____

How was I favored/How did I show favor? (Favor)

_____
_____
_____
_____

_____

_____

_____

What have I done to secure my future/What are My goals? (Future)

_____

_____

_____

_____

_____

_____

_____

How have I stood firm in my walk and words? (Foundation/Walk/ Talk)

_____

_____

_____

_____

_____

_____

_____

How have I displayed Christ's attitude/Where can I improve? (Attitude)

_____

_____

_____

_____

_____

_____

_____

What Have I listened to that has stood out? (Hear)

_____

_____

_____

_____

_____

_____

What have I accomplished? (Do)

_____

_____

_____

_____

_____

_____

How have I changed/am changing? (Convicted/Challenged/ Changed)

_____

_____

_____

_____

_____

_____

Date ___/___/___

Today I am a Child of God

Write a proclamation of belief. Each time you write, you are ensuring your vision and beliefs will carry on to the next generation.

_____

_____

_____

_____

_____

_____

_____

_____

_____

_____

How has my belief dictated my behavior today? (Faith)

_____

_____

_____

_____

_____

_____

_____

How was I favored/How did I show favor? (Favor)

_____

_____

_____

_____

_____

_____

_____

What have I done to secure my future/What are My goals?
(Future)

_____

_____

_____

_____

_____

_____

_____

How have I stood firm in my walk and words? (Foundation/Walk/
Talk)

_____

_____

_____

_____

_____

_____

How have I displayed Christ's attitude/Where can I improve?
(Attitude)

_____

_____

_____

_____

_____

_____

_____

What Have I listened to that has stood out? (Hear)

_____

_____

_____

_____

_____

_____

What have I accomplished? (Do)

_____

_____

_____

_____

_____

_____

How have I changed/am changing? (Convicted/Challenged/Changed)

_____

_____

_____

_____

_____

_____

Date ___/___/___

Today I am a Child of God

Write a proclamation of belief. Each time you write, you are ensuring your vision and beliefs will carry on to the next generation.

_____
_____
_____
_____
_____
_____
_____
_____
_____

How has my belief dictated my behavior today? (Faith)

_____
_____
_____
_____
_____
_____

How was I favored/How did I show favor? (Favor)

_____
_____
_____
_____

_____

_____

_____

What have I done to secure my future/What are My goals?
(Future)

_____

_____

_____

_____

_____

_____

_____

How have I stood firm in my walk and words? (Foundation/Walk/
Talk)

_____

_____

_____

_____

_____

_____

_____

How have I displayed Christ's attitude/Where can I improve?
(Attitude)

_____

_____

_____

_____

_____

_____

_____

What Have I listened to that has stood out? (Hear)

_____

_____

_____

_____

_____

_____

What have I accomplished? (Do)

_____

_____

_____

_____

_____

_____

How have I changed/am changing? (Convicted/Challenged/ Changed)

_____

_____

_____

_____

_____

_____

Date ___/___/___

Today I am a Child of God

Write a proclamation of belief. Each time you write, you are ensuring your vision and beliefs will carry on to the next generation.

_____

_____

_____

_____

_____

_____

_____

_____

_____

How has my belief dictated my behavior today? (Faith)

_____

_____

_____

_____

_____

_____

How was I favored/How did I show favor? (Favor)

_____

_____

_____

_____
_____
_____

What have I done to secure my future/What are My goals?
(Future)

_____
_____
_____
_____
_____
_____
_____

How have I stood firm in my walk and words? (Foundation/Walk/
Talk)

_____
_____
_____
_____
_____
_____
_____

How have I displayed Christ's attitude/Where can I improve?
(Attitude)

_____
_____
_____
_____
_____

_____

_____

What Have I listened to that has stood out? (Hear)

_____

_____

_____

_____

_____

_____

What have I accomplished? (Do)

_____

_____

_____

_____

_____

_____

*How have I changed/am changing? (Convicted/Challenged/
Changed)*

_____

_____

_____

_____

_____

_____

Date ___/___/___

Today I am a Child of God

Write a proclamation of belief. Each time you write, you are ensuring your vision and beliefs will carry on to the next generation.

_____
_____
_____
_____
_____
_____
_____
_____
_____
_____

How has my belief dictated my behavior today? (Faith)

_____
_____
_____
_____
_____
_____

How was I favored/How did I show favor? (Favor)

_____
_____
_____
_____

_____
_____
_____

What have I done to secure my future/What are My goals? (Future)

_____
_____
_____
_____
_____
_____
_____

How have I stood firm in my walk and words? (Foundation/Walk/ Talk)

_____
_____
_____
_____
_____
_____
_____

How have I displayed Christ's attitude/Where can I improve? (Attitude)

_____
_____
_____
_____
_____

_____
_____

What Have I listened to that has stood out? (Hear)

_____
_____
_____
_____
_____
_____

What have I accomplished? (Do)

_____
_____
_____
_____
_____
_____

How have I changed/am changing? (Convicted/Challenged/ Changed)

_____
_____
_____
_____
_____
_____

Date ___/___/___

Today I am a Child of God

Write a proclamation of belief. Each time you write, you are ensuring your vision and beliefs will carry on to the next generation.

_____

_____

_____

_____

_____

_____

_____

_____

_____

_____

How has my belief dictated my behavior today? (Faith)

_____

_____

_____

_____

_____

_____

How was I favored/How did I show favor? (Favor)

_____

_____

_____

_____

_____

_____

What have I done to secure my future/What are My goals?
(Future)

_____

_____

_____

_____

_____

_____

How have I stood firm in my walk and words? (Foundation/Walk/
Talk)

_____

_____

_____

_____

_____

_____

How have I displayed Christ's attitude/Where can I improve?
(Attitude)

_____

_____

_____

_____

_____

_____

What Have I listened to that has stood out? (Hear)

_____

_____

_____

_____

_____

_____

_____

What have I accomplished? (Do)

_____

_____

_____

_____

_____

_____

_____

How have I changed/am changing? (Convicted/Challenged/Changed)

_____

_____

_____

_____

_____

_____

_____

Date ___/___/___

Today I am a Child of God

Write a proclamation of belief. Each time you write, you are ensuring your vision and beliefs will carry on to the next generation.

_____
_____
_____
_____
_____
_____
_____
_____
_____
_____

How has my belief dictated my behavior today? (Faith)

_____
_____
_____
_____
_____
_____

How was I favored/How did I show favor? (Favor)

_____
_____
_____
_____

_____
_____
_____

What have I done to secure my future/What are My goals? (Future)

_____
_____
_____
_____
_____
_____
_____

How have I stood firm in my walk and words? (Foundation/Walk/ Talk)

_____
_____
_____
_____
_____
_____
_____

How have I displayed Christ's attitude/Where can I improve? (Attitude)

_____
_____
_____
_____
_____

_____

_____

What Have I listened to that has stood out? (Hear)

_____

_____

_____

_____

_____

_____

_____

What have I accomplished? (Do)

_____

_____

_____

_____

_____

_____

How have I changed/am changing? (Convicted/Challenged/Changed)

_____

_____

_____

_____

_____

_____

Date ___/___/___

Today I am a Child of God

Write a proclamation of belief. Each time you write, you are ensuring your vision and beliefs will carry on to the next generation.

_____

_____

_____

_____

_____

_____

_____

_____

_____

_____

How has my belief dictated my behavior today? (Faith)

_____

_____

_____

_____

_____

_____

How was I favored/How did I show favor? (Favor)

_____

_____

_____

_____

_____
_____
_____

What have I done to secure my future/What are My goals? (Future)

_____
_____
_____
_____
_____
_____

How have I stood firm in my walk and words? (Foundation/Walk/ Talk)

_____
_____
_____
_____
_____
_____

How have I displayed Christ's attitude/Where can I improve? (Attitude)

_____
_____
_____
_____

_____

_____

What Have I listened to that has stood out? (Hear)

_____

_____

_____

_____

_____

_____

What have I accomplished? (Do)

_____

_____

_____

_____

_____

_____

How have I changed/am changing? (Convicted/Challenged/Changed)

_____

_____

_____

_____

_____

_____

Date ___/___/___

Today I am a Child of God

Write a proclamation of belief. Each time you write, you are ensuring your vision and beliefs will carry on to the next generation.

_____
_____
_____
_____
_____
_____
_____
_____
_____
_____

How has my belief dictated my behavior today? (Faith)

_____
_____
_____
_____
_____
_____

How was I favored/How did I show favor? (Favor)

_____
_____
_____
_____

_____

_____

_____

What have I done to secure my future/What are My goals? (Future)

_____

_____

_____

_____

_____

_____

_____

How have I stood firm in my walk and words? (Foundation/Walk/ Talk)

_____

_____

_____

_____

_____

_____

How have I displayed Christ's attitude/Where can I improve? (Attitude)

_____

_____

_____

_____

_____
_____

What Have I listened to that has stood out? (Hear)

_____
_____
_____
_____
_____
_____
_____

What have I accomplished? (Do)

_____
_____
_____
_____
_____
_____

How have I changed/am changing? (Convicted/Challenged/ Changed)

_____
_____
_____
_____
_____
_____
_____

Date ___/___/___

Today I am a Child of God

Write a proclamation of belief. Each time you write, you are ensuring your vision and beliefs will carry on to the next generation.

_____

_____

_____

_____

_____

_____

_____

_____

_____

How has my belief dictated my behavior today? (Faith)

_____

_____

_____

_____

_____

_____

How was I favored/How did I show favor? (Favor)

_____

_____

_____

_____

_____

_____

_____

What have I done to secure my future/What are My goals?
(Future)

_____

_____

_____

_____

_____

_____

_____

How have I stood firm in my walk and words? (Foundation/Walk/
Talk)

_____

_____

_____

_____

_____

_____

_____

How have I displayed Christ's attitude/Where can I improve?
(Attitude)

_____

_____

_____

_____

What Have I listened to that has stood out? (Hear)

_____

_____

_____

_____

_____

_____

What have I accomplished? (Do)

_____

_____

_____

_____

_____

_____

How have I changed/am changing? (Convicted/Challenged/ Changed)

_____

_____

_____

_____

_____

_____

Date ___/___/___

Today I am a Child of God

Write a proclamation of belief. Each time you write, you are ensuring your vision and beliefs will carry on to the next generation.

_____

_____

_____

_____

_____

_____

_____

_____

_____

_____

How has my belief dictated my behavior today? (Faith)

_____

_____

_____

_____

_____

_____

How was I favored/How did I show favor? (Favor)

_____

_____

_____

_____

_____

_____

_____

What have I done to secure my future/What are My goals? (Future)

_____

_____

_____

_____

_____

_____

_____

How have I stood firm in my walk and words? (Foundation/Walk/ Talk)

_____

_____

_____

_____

_____

_____

_____

How have I displayed Christ's attitude/Where can I improve? (Attitude)

_____

_____

_____

_____

_____

_____
_____

What Have I listened to that has stood out? (Hear)

_____
_____
_____
_____
_____
_____

What have I accomplished? (Do)

_____
_____
_____
_____
_____
_____

How have I changed/am changing? (Convicted/Challenged/ Changed)

_____
_____
_____
_____
_____
_____

Date ___/___/___

Today I am a Child of God

Write a proclamation of belief. Each time you write, you are ensuring your vision and beliefs will carry on to the next generation.

_____

_____

_____

_____

_____

_____

_____

_____

_____

How has my belief dictated my behavior today? (Faith)

_____

_____

_____

_____

_____

_____

How was I favored/How did I show favor? (Favor)

_____

_____

_____

_____

_____
_____
_____

What have I done to secure my future/What are My goals? (Future)

_____
_____
_____
_____
_____
_____

How have I stood firm in my walk and words? (Foundation/Walk/ Talk)

_____
_____
_____
_____
_____
_____

How have I displayed Christ's attitude/Where can I improve? (Attitude)

_____
_____
_____
_____

_____

_____

What Have I listened to that has stood out? (Hear)

_____

_____

_____

_____

_____

_____

What have I accomplished? (Do)

_____

_____

_____

_____

_____

_____

How have I changed/am changing? (Convicted/Challenged/ Changed)

_____

_____

_____

_____

_____

_____

Date ___/___/___

Today I am a Child of God

Write a proclamation of belief. Each time you write, you are ensuring your vision and beliefs will carry on to the next generation.

_____
_____
_____
_____
_____
_____
_____
_____
_____
_____

How has my belief dictated my behavior today? (Faith)

_____
_____
_____
_____
_____
_____

How was I favored/How did I show favor? (Favor)

_____
_____
_____
_____

_____
_____
_____

What have I done to secure my future/What are My goals?
(Future)

_____
_____
_____
_____
_____
_____
_____

How have I stood firm in my walk and words? (Foundation/Walk/
Talk)

_____
_____
_____
_____
_____
_____
_____

How have I displayed Christ's attitude/Where can I improve?
(Attitude)

_____
_____
_____
_____
_____

_____
_____

What Have I listened to that has stood out? (Hear)

_____
_____
_____
_____
_____
_____

What have I accomplished? (Do)

_____
_____
_____
_____
_____
_____

How have I changed/am changing? (Convicted/Challenged/Changed)

_____
_____
_____
_____
_____
_____

Date ___/___/___

Today I am a Child of God

Write a proclamation of belief. Each time you write, you are ensuring your vision and beliefs will carry on to the next generation.

_____
_____
_____
_____
_____
_____
_____
_____
_____
_____

How has my belief dictated my behavior today? (Faith)

_____
_____
_____
_____
_____
_____
_____

How was I favored/How did I show favor? (Favor)

_____
_____
_____
_____

_____

_____

_____

What have I done to secure my future/What are My goals?
(Future)

_____

_____

_____

_____

_____

_____

_____

How have I stood firm in my walk and words? (Foundation/Walk/
Talk)

_____

_____

_____

_____

_____

_____

_____

How have I displayed Christ's attitude/Where can I improve?
(Attitude)

_____

_____

_____

_____

_____

_____

_____

What Have I listened to that has stood out? (Hear)

_____

_____

_____

_____

_____

_____

What have I accomplished? (Do)

_____

_____

_____

_____

_____

_____

How have I changed/am changing? (Convicted/Challenged/Changed)

_____

_____

_____

_____

_____

_____

Date ___/___/___

Today I am a Child of God

Write a proclamation of belief. Each time you write, you are ensuring your vision and beliefs will carry on to the next generation.

_____
_____
_____
_____
_____
_____
_____
_____
_____

How has my belief dictated my behavior today? (Faith)

_____
_____
_____
_____
_____
_____

How was I favored/How did I show favor? (Favor)

_____
_____
_____
_____

_____
_____
_____

What have I done to secure my future/What are My goals?
(Future)

_____
_____
_____
_____
_____
_____

How have I stood firm in my walk and words? (Foundation/Walk/
Talk)

_____
_____
_____
_____
_____
_____

How have I displayed Christ's attitude/Where can I improve?
(Attitude)

_____
_____
_____
_____
_____

_____

_____

What Have I listened to that has stood out? (Hear)

_____

_____

_____

_____

_____

_____

What have I accomplished? (Do)

_____

_____

_____

_____

_____

_____

How have I changed/am changing? (Convicted/Challenged/ Changed)

_____

_____

_____

_____

_____

_____

Date ___/___/___

Today I am a Child of God

Write a proclamation of belief. Each time you write, you are ensuring your vision and beliefs will carry on to the next generation.

_____
_____
_____
_____
_____
_____
_____
_____
_____

How has my belief dictated my behavior today? (Faith)

_____
_____
_____
_____
_____
_____

How was I favored/How did I show favor? (Favor)

_____
_____
_____
_____

_____
_____
_____

What have I done to secure my future/What are My goals?
(Future)

_____
_____
_____
_____
_____
_____

How have I stood firm in my walk and words? (Foundation/Walk/
Talk)

_____
_____
_____
_____
_____
_____

How have I displayed Christ's attitude/Where can I improve?
(Attitude)

_____
_____
_____
_____

_____
_____

What Have I listened to that has stood out? (Hear)

_____
_____
_____
_____
_____
_____
_____

What have I accomplished? (Do)

_____
_____
_____
_____
_____
_____
_____

How have I changed/am changing? (Convicted/Challenged/Changed)

_____
_____
_____
_____
_____
_____
_____

Date ___/___/___

Today I am a Child of God

Write a proclamation of belief. Each time you write, you are ensuring your vision and beliefs will carry on to the next generation.

_____
_____
_____
_____
_____
_____
_____
_____
_____
_____

How has my belief dictated my behavior today? (Faith)

_____
_____
_____
_____
_____
_____

How was I favored/How did I show favor? (Favor)

_____
_____
_____
_____

_____

_____

_____

What have I done to secure my future/What are My goals? (Future)

_____

_____

_____

_____

_____

_____

How have I stood firm in my walk and words? (Foundation/Walk/ Talk)

_____

_____

_____

_____

_____

_____

How have I displayed Christ's attitude/Where can I improve? (Attitude)

_____

_____

_____

_____

_____

_____

_____

What Have I listened to that has stood out? (Hear)

_____

_____

_____

_____

_____

_____

What have I accomplished? (Do)

_____

_____

_____

_____

_____

_____

How have I changed/am changing? (Convicted/Challenged/ Changed)

_____

_____

_____

_____

_____

_____

Date ___/___/___

Today I am a Child of God

Write a proclamation of belief. Each time you write, you are ensuring your vision and beliefs will carry on to the next generation.

_____

_____

_____

_____

_____

_____

_____

_____

_____

How has my belief dictated my behavior today? (Faith)

_____

_____

_____

_____

_____

_____

How was I favored/How did I show favor? (Favor)

_____

_____

_____

_____
_____
_____

What have I done to secure my future/What are My goals? (Future)

_____
_____
_____
_____
_____
_____
_____

How have I stood firm in my walk and words? (Foundation/Walk/ Talk)

_____
_____
_____
_____
_____
_____
_____

How have I displayed Christ's attitude/Where can I improve? (Attitude)

_____
_____
_____
_____
_____

_____

_____

What Have I listened to that has stood out? (Hear)

_____

_____

_____

_____

_____

_____

What have I accomplished? (Do)

_____

_____

_____

_____

_____

_____

How have I changed/am changing? (Convicted/Challenged/
Changed)

_____

_____

_____

_____

_____

_____

Date ___/___/___

Today I am a Child of God

Write a proclamation of belief. Each time you write, you are ensuring your vision and beliefs will carry on to the next generation.

_____
_____
_____
_____
_____
_____
_____
_____
_____
_____

How has my belief dictated my behavior today? (Faith)

_____
_____
_____
_____
_____
_____

How was I favored/How did I show favor? (Favor)

_____
_____
_____
_____

_____
_____
_____

What have I done to secure my future/What are My goals? (Future)

_____
_____
_____
_____
_____
_____
_____

How have I stood firm in my walk and words? (Foundation/Walk/ Talk)

_____
_____
_____
_____
_____
_____
_____

How have I displayed Christ's attitude/Where can I improve? (Attitude)

_____
_____
_____
_____
_____

_____
_____

What Have I listened to that has stood out? (Hear)

_____
_____
_____
_____
_____
_____
_____

What have I accomplished? (Do)

_____
_____
_____
_____
_____
_____
_____

How have I changed/am changing? (Convicted/Challenged/Changed)

_____
_____
_____
_____
_____
_____
_____

Date ___/___/___

Today I am a Child of God

Write a proclamation of belief. Each time you write, you are ensuring your vision and beliefs will carry on to the next generation.

_____

_____

_____

_____

_____

_____

_____

_____

_____

_____

How has my belief dictated my behavior today? (Faith)

_____

_____

_____

_____

_____

_____

_____

How was I favored/How did I show favor? (Favor)

_____

_____

_____

_____

_____

_____

_____

What have I done to secure my future/What are My goals?
(Future)

_____

_____

_____

_____

_____

_____

How have I stood firm in my walk and words? (Foundation/Walk/
Talk)

_____

_____

_____

_____

_____

_____

How have I displayed Christ's attitude/Where can I improve?
(Attitude)

_____

_____

_____

_____

_____
_____

What Have I listened to that has stood out? (Hear)

_____
_____
_____
_____
_____
_____

What have I accomplished? (Do)

_____
_____
_____
_____
_____
_____

How have I changed/am changing? (Convicted/Challenged/ Changed)

_____
_____
_____
_____
_____
_____

Date ___/___/___

Today I am a Child of God

Write a proclamation of belief. Each time you write, you are ensuring your vision and beliefs will carry on to the next generation.

_____

_____

_____

_____

_____

_____

_____

_____

_____

_____

How has my belief dictated my behavior today? (Faith)

_____

_____

_____

_____

_____

_____

How was I favored/How did I show favor? (Favor)

_____

_____

_____

_____

_____

_____

What have I done to secure my future/What are My goals? (Future)

_____

_____

_____

_____

_____

_____

_____

How have I stood firm in my walk and words? (Foundation/Walk/ Talk)

_____

_____

_____

_____

_____

_____

_____

How have I displayed Christ's attitude/Where can I improve? (Attitude)

_____

_____

_____

_____

_____

_____
_____

What Have I listened to that has stood out? (Hear)

_____
_____
_____
_____
_____
_____
_____

What have I accomplished? (Do)

_____
_____
_____
_____
_____
_____
_____

How have I changed/am changing? (Convicted/Challenged/Changed)

_____
_____
_____
_____
_____
_____
_____

Date ___/___/___

Today I am a Child of God

Write a proclamation of belief. Each time you write, you are ensuring your vision and beliefs will carry on to the next generation.

_____
_____
_____
_____
_____
_____
_____
_____
_____
_____

How has my belief dictated my behavior today? (Faith)

_____
_____
_____
_____
_____
_____
_____

How was I favored/How did I show favor? (Favor)

_____
_____
_____
_____

_____

_____

_____

What have I done to secure my future/What are My goals? (Future)

_____

_____

_____

_____

_____

_____

_____

How have I stood firm in my walk and words? (Foundation/Walk/ Talk)

_____

_____

_____

_____

_____

_____

_____

How have I displayed Christ's attitude/Where can I improve? (Attitude)

_____

_____

_____

_____

_____

_____

_____

What Have I listened to that has stood out? (Hear)

_____

_____

_____

_____

_____

_____

What have I accomplished? (Do)

_____

_____

_____

_____

_____

_____

How have I changed/am changing? (Convicted/Challenged/Changed)

_____

_____

_____

_____

_____

_____

Date ___/___/___

Today I am a Child of God

Write a proclamation of belief. Each time you write, you are ensuring your vision and beliefs will carry on to the next generation.

_____
_____
_____
_____
_____
_____
_____
_____
_____
_____

How has my belief dictated my behavior today? (Faith)

_____
_____
_____
_____
_____
_____
_____

How was I favored/How did I show favor? (Favor)

_____
_____
_____
_____

_____
_____
_____

What have I done to secure my future/What are My goals? (Future)

_____
_____
_____
_____
_____
_____
_____

How have I stood firm in my walk and words? (Foundation/Walk/ Talk)

_____
_____
_____
_____
_____
_____

How have I displayed Christ's attitude/Where can I improve? (Attitude)

_____
_____
_____
_____
_____

_____
_____

What Have I listened to that has stood out? (Hear)

_____
_____
_____
_____
_____
_____

What have I accomplished? (Do)

_____
_____
_____
_____
_____
_____

How have I changed/am changing? (Convicted/Challenged/ Changed)

_____
_____
_____
_____
_____
_____

Date ___/___/___

Today I am a Child of God

Write a proclamation of belief. Each time you write, you are ensuring your vision and beliefs will carry on to the next generation.

_____
_____
_____
_____
_____
_____
_____
_____
_____

How has my belief dictated my behavior today? (Faith)

_____
_____
_____
_____
_____
_____

How was I favored/How did I show favor? (Favor)

_____
_____
_____

_____

_____

_____

What have I done to secure my future/What are My goals? (Future)

_____

_____

_____

_____

_____

_____

_____

How have I stood firm in my walk and words? (Foundation/Walk/ Talk)

_____

_____

_____

_____

_____

_____

_____

How have I displayed Christ's attitude/Where can I improve? (Attitude)

_____

_____

_____

_____

_____

_____
_____

What Have I listened to that has stood out? (Hear)

_____
_____
_____
_____
_____
_____

What have I accomplished? (Do)

_____
_____
_____
_____
_____
_____

How have I changed/am changing? (Convicted/Challenged/ Changed)

_____
_____
_____
_____
_____
_____

Date ___/___/___

Today I am a Child of God

Write a proclamation of belief. Each time you write, you are ensuring your vision and beliefs will carry on to the next generation.

_____
_____
_____
_____
_____
_____
_____
_____
_____
_____

How has my belief dictated my behavior today? (Faith)

_____
_____
_____
_____
_____
_____

How was I favored/How did I show favor? (Favor)

_____
_____
_____
_____

_____

_____

_____

What have I done to secure my future/What are My goals?
(Future)

_____

_____

_____

_____

_____

_____

_____

How have I stood firm in my walk and words? (Foundation/Walk/
Talk)

_____

_____

_____

_____

_____

_____

_____

How have I displayed Christ's attitude/Where can I improve?
(Attitude)

_____

_____

_____

_____

_____

_____

_____

What Have I listened to that has stood out? (Hear)

_____

_____

_____

_____

_____

_____

What have I accomplished? (Do)

_____

_____

_____

_____

_____

_____

How have I changed/am changing? (Convicted/Challenged/Changed)

_____

_____

_____

_____

_____

_____

Date ___/___/___

Today I am a Child of God

Write a proclamation of belief. Each time you write, you are ensuring your vision and beliefs will carry on to the next generation.

_____

_____

_____

_____

_____

_____

_____

_____

_____

How has my belief dictated my behavior today? (Faith)

_____

_____

_____

_____

_____

_____

How was I favored/How did I show favor? (Favor)

_____

_____

_____

_____

_____

_____

_____

What have I done to secure my future/What are My goals? (Future)

_____

_____

_____

_____

_____

_____

How have I stood firm in my walk and words? (Foundation/Walk/ Talk)

_____

_____

_____

_____

_____

_____

How have I displayed Christ's attitude/Where can I improve? (Attitude)

_____

_____

_____

_____

_____

_____
_____

What Have I listened to that has stood out? (Hear)

_____
_____
_____
_____
_____
_____

What have I accomplished? (Do)

_____
_____
_____
_____
_____
_____

How have I changed/am changing? (Convicted/Challenged/ Changed)

_____
_____
_____
_____
_____
_____

Date ___/___/___

Today I am a Child of God

Write a proclamation of belief. Each time you write, you are ensuring your vision and beliefs will carry on to the next generation.

_____
_____
_____
_____
_____
_____
_____
_____
_____

How has my belief dictated my behavior today? (Faith)

_____
_____
_____
_____
_____
_____

How was I favored/How did I show favor? (Favor)

_____
_____
_____
_____

_____

_____

_____

What have I done to secure my future/What are My goals?
(Future)

_____

_____

_____

_____

_____

_____

_____

How have I stood firm in my walk and words? (Foundation/Walk/
Talk)

_____

_____

_____

_____

_____

_____

_____

How have I displayed Christ's attitude/Where can I improve?
(Attitude)

_____

_____

_____

_____

_____

_____
_____

What Have I listened to that has stood out? (Hear)

_____
_____
_____
_____
_____
_____
_____

What have I accomplished? (Do)

_____
_____
_____
_____
_____
_____
_____

How have I changed/am changing? (Convicted/Challenged/Changed)

_____
_____
_____
_____
_____
_____
_____

Date ___/___/___

Today I am a Child of God

Write a proclamation of belief. Each time you write, you are ensuring your vision and beliefs will carry on to the next generation.

_____

_____

_____

_____

_____

_____

_____

_____

_____

How has my belief dictated my behavior today? (Faith)

_____

_____

_____

_____

_____

_____

How was I favored/How did I show favor? (Favor)

_____

_____

_____

_____
_____
_____

What have I done to secure my future/What are My goals?
(Future)

_____
_____
_____
_____
_____
_____
_____

How have I stood firm in my walk and words? (Foundation/Walk/
Talk)

_____
_____
_____
_____
_____
_____

How have I displayed Christ's attitude/Where can I improve?
(Attitude)

_____
_____
_____
_____

_____

_____

What Have I listened to that has stood out? (Hear)

_____

_____

_____

_____

_____

_____

_____

What have I accomplished? (Do)

_____

_____

_____

_____

_____

_____

_____

How have I changed/am changing? (Convicted/Challenged/ Changed)

_____

_____

_____

_____

_____

_____

_____

Date ___/___/___

Today I am a Child of God

Write a proclamation of belief. Each time you write, you are ensuring your vision and beliefs will carry on to the next generation.

_____
_____
_____
_____
_____
_____
_____
_____
_____
_____

How has my belief dictated my behavior today? (Faith)

_____
_____
_____
_____
_____
_____
_____

How was I favored/How did I show favor? (Favor)

_____
_____
_____
_____

_____

_____

_____

What have I done to secure my future/What are My goals? (Future)

_____

_____

_____

_____

_____

_____

_____

How have I stood firm in my walk and words? (Foundation/Walk/ Talk)

_____

_____

_____

_____

_____

_____

_____

How have I displayed Christ's attitude/Where can I improve? (Attitude)

_____

_____

_____

_____

_____

_____

_____

What Have I listened to that has stood out? (Hear)

_____

_____

_____

_____

_____

_____

What have I accomplished? (Do)

_____

_____

_____

_____

_____

_____

How have I changed/am changing? (Convicted/Challenged/ Changed)

_____

_____

_____

_____

_____

_____

Date ___/___/___

Today I am a Child of God

Write a proclamation of belief. Each time you write, you are ensuring your vision and beliefs will carry on to the next generation.

_____

_____

_____

_____

_____

_____

_____

_____

_____

_____

How has my belief dictated my behavior today? (Faith)

_____

_____

_____

_____

_____

_____

How was I favored/How did I show favor? (Favor)

_____

_____

_____

_____

_____

_____

_____

What have I done to secure my future/What are My goals? (Future)

_____

_____

_____

_____

_____

_____

_____

How have I stood firm in my walk and words? (Foundation/Walk/ Talk)

_____

_____

_____

_____

_____

_____

_____

How have I displayed Christ's attitude/Where can I improve? (Attitude)

_____

_____

_____

_____

_____

_____
_____

What Have I listened to that has stood out? (Hear)

_____
_____
_____
_____
_____
_____

What have I accomplished? (Do)

_____
_____
_____
_____
_____
_____

How have I changed/am changing? (Convicted/Challenged/
Changed)

_____
_____
_____
_____
_____
_____

Date ___/___/___

Today I am a Child of God

Write a proclamation of belief. Each time you write, you are ensuring your vision and beliefs will carry on to the next generation.

_____
_____
_____
_____
_____
_____
_____
_____
_____
_____

How has my belief dictated my behavior today? (Faith)

_____
_____
_____
_____
_____
_____

How was I favored/How did I show favor? (Favor)

_____
_____
_____
_____

_____

_____

_____

What have I done to secure my future/What are My goals?
(Future)

_____

_____

_____

_____

_____

_____

_____

How have I stood firm in my walk and words? (Foundation/Walk/
Talk)

_____

_____

_____

_____

_____

_____

_____

How have I displayed Christ's attitude/Where can I improve?
(Attitude)

_____

_____

_____

_____

_____

_____

_____

What Have I listened to that has stood out? (Hear)

_____

_____

_____

_____

_____

_____

_____

What have I accomplished? (Do)

_____

_____

_____

_____

_____

_____

_____

How have I changed/am changing? (Convicted/Challenged/ Changed)

_____

_____

_____

_____

_____

_____

_____

Today I am a child of God

I have Faith to Move Mountains

Favor from the King of Kings

And and Future that is out of this World

My Foundation is the Word of God

My Walk is Sure

My Talk is Confident

My Attitude is Like Christ's

Today I will Hear the Word of God

Today I will Do the Will of god

Today I am Convicted, Challenged and Changed

In Jesus Name,

Amen